An Apple
A Day

An Apple A Day

A Heartwarming Collection of True Horse Stories

Compiled and Edited by Kimberly Gatto

Foreword by Margie Goldstein Engle

With stories by Kathy Connelly, Max Gahwyler, Cooky McClung, and many others

An Apple A Day:
A Heartwarming Collection of True Horse Stories
© 2000 Kimberly Gatto

Published in the United States of America by
Half Halt Press, Inc.
P. O. Box 67, Boonsboro, MD 21713
www.halfhaltpress.com

Cover and interior design by Design Point, Epping, NH
Cover photo by Debbie Bishop, Hoofbeats Photos
Editorial Services by Samantha Harrison

Printed in The United States of America

Library of Congress Cataloging-in-Publication Data

An apple a day : a heartwarming collection of true horse stories
/ compiled and edited by Kimberly Gatto ; foreword by Margie
Goldstein Engle ; with stories by Kathy Connelly, Max
Gahwyler, Cooky McClung, and many others.
    p. cm.
  ISBN 0-939481-57-X (paperback)
    1. Horses--Anecdotes. I. Gatto, Kimberly

  SF301 .A72 2000
  636.1--dc21   00-061368

For my mom, Ann Gatto,
who has always believed in me
as a rider, writer, daughter
and friend.

K.A.G.

TABLE OF CONTENTS

Foreword

Winston Churchill said it best: "There is something about the outside of a horse that is good for the inside of a man." He was right. **An Apple A Day** celebrates this unique connection that human beings share with horses.

Even as a child, I felt that special bond with the horses and ponies that I rode and those that my friends rode. They were our friends. They knew how we were feeling and could always tell our emotions at the time. When we were sad, they seemed to understand and almost try to sympathize with us in their own way. When we were playful, they responded in kind. And later, when I began competing, if I felt confident, they felt the same way.

In show jumping, the connection between horse and rider has to be extremely close. Both horse and rider need to know what each body signal means, which aids or equipment work best with each horse, and which type of training methods work best on each. You have to deal with each horse as a complete individual just as you would with a child. When worked with correctly, the rewards are amazing!

Horses give so much to humans with a selfless love and trust that is awe-inspiring. It is important to never give them reason to destroy that trust. I think sometimes all of us take their abilities, love, and pure heart for granted, and we need to be reminded of all they do for us. When they give you even more than you think is possible—such as clearing a seven foot, seven inch wall, or jumping their first 18 inch hurdle—the feeling defies words. They are so eager to learn and please, and we need to reward and credit them for this.

Horses have helped mankind since the beginning of time in everything from transportation, to farming, to offering love and companionship as a pet. They have aided the handicapped in ways that seem like miracles, such as helping both physically and psychologically impaired individuals. The list goes on and on.

Working with the different personalities of each horse makes it interesting. It's not like working with a baseball bat or a tennis racquet or some other inanimate object. I think it's important to appreciate horses for who and what they represent. I believe the stories in **An Apple A Day** remind us of some of the many ways horses warm our hearts. When you read these tales, you will delight in them, as well as recall your own vivid memories of your favorite horse or pony. ☾

Margie Goldstein Engle
USET Team Member, Six-time AGA Rider of the Year

The horse is
God's gift to mankind.

Arab proverb

What Horses and Sculpture Have in Common

By Kathy Connelly

Michelangelo said that the sculpture was already contained in the marble. You just had to know what pieces of marble to take away. So it is with horses. Their talent, grace and beauty are already contained in their bodies and are expressed through their soul and spirit. We just have to learn how to bring out each horse's talent while keeping intact the individuality of his soul and the sparkle of his spirit.

That is why Xenophon, in his writings on training,

spoke of "gentling" the horses. To me the words of Michelangelo and Xenophon evoke feelings of softness and kindness guided by having a purpose and expressing it with clarity. If you wield clumsily a dull bladed ax rather than deftly employ a finely crafted artisan's chisel to a piece of marble, the result is vastly different. One result looks like an instrument of torture was used and the other piece of marble looks like a magic wand touched it. Michelangelo saw the marble and listened to it, and the marble told him what to do.

Horses are like children. They cannot defend themselves nor should they ever have to. It is our responsibility as trainers to be clear enough and firm enough but kind; to leave each horse with his dignity at the end of each session so that we can develop in him the desire to still try tomorrow. Heather St. Clair Davis summed it up beautifully once when she said, "How can I expect my friend to give me his poetry to read if all I do is correct his spelling?"

This is what we must do for the horse. Watch him and really see him and then listen and he will show us how to train him. Most "resistance," as we term it, comes because the horse does not understand and we need to be clearer. I have learned so much from all of my horses. The generosity of the horse's spirit is infinite and the courage in his heart is awe-inspiring.

As a USPC "A" rider, I competed in a three-day event in Australia when I was nineteen. It was a very exciting experience as the Australians are fearless and their cross-country courses test to the superlative the rider's and horse's mettle. I have been fortunate to event some very courageous horses, and at nineteen was the U.S. three-day event Champion for the USPC.

I thought I knew what courage was in a horse from those experiences, until I felt, years later, the most moving feeling of courage in two horses that I had ever experienced. These horses were Gabrielle and Enterprise.

Gabrielle was an elegant and beautiful FEI mare that I competed. She was truly claustrophobic about entering dressage arena stadiums and with crowds, would panic, freeze, rear and run backwards. She would even try to jump over or run into the other horses if they were in her way to avoid entering that stadium atmosphere. From her I learned patience, because inside of her was a horse that really did want to go in but didn't know how and she didn't know that she would be all right in there. I had to learn what she was thinking and not only be her psychologist but also her cheerleader! I spent much time with her to teach her that she could do it and be okay. I took her to the United States Dressage Championships. I was warned not to take her because she would not enter the stadium. I sat in the saddle and felt her go into her blind panic. I had done a lot of psychological "arena entry" work with her and somewhere in her heart she found the courage to go into the arena. She learned to overcome her fear and became the U.S. Intermediare I Freestyle Champion and U.S. Reserve Champion, Prix St. Georges and Intermediare I. I don't know the words to describe the feeling of a horse trusting you that much and loving you back the way that they have to love.

When I first saw my horse Enterprise, he was thin, with long hair and he looked sad. There was no light in his eyes. He would hover in the back of the stall with his hind end to the door. It was dangerous to go into his stall because he would attack you, trying to kick and bite. He was about fourth level when I tried him. When I tried him he was difficult but powerful, and I felt that underneath there was brilliance in his spirit that needed to find a way out. He had something special.

Years later I found out that he has been thought so

difficult and bad at home that he had never been shown. Many a rider apparently had hit the dirt as a result of his lightning quick, twisting bucks. Sadly, the result was that often at night his rider would go in his stall and beat him, several times severely. Then he was sent on his way to a dealer's barn.

He taught me a great deal about what great courage lies in a horse's heart. He was a very exuberant horse with tremendous energy. He just needed help channeling it the right way. I spent much time with him and much thought on how to help him overcome his fears. I learned so much from him. Through his courage, he learned to trust me. In 2 1/2 years he was U.S. Grand Prix Freestyle Champion and in 3 1/2 years he was U.S. Grand Prix World Cup Champion and then went on to train in Europe.

What I personally did was not special. Many people have done with their horses what I have done. What is special is what lies in the heart of a horse.

I have found the magnitude of their spirits to be inspirational and humbling beyond measure. When you are riding a horse in this kind of drama and partnership, there is a magic that happens which changes and reshapes your soul. I have to say that the courage and generosity that I have experienced from my horses has changed my horizons forever. ♘

Kathy Connelly, international dressage rider, trainer, and coach, has represented the U.S. team at the World Cup in Sweden. She was U.S. Grand Prix Freestyle Champion and U.S. World Cup Champion. Kathy has coached many riders to victory, including the silver medallist at the 1999 Pan Am Games. She resides at her farm, Apple Valley Farm, in Harvard, Massachusetts during the summer and in Wellington, Florida in the winter.

Story reprinted by permission of Golden Hills Press and Kathy Connelly

The Naming
of Tommy

By Nancy Pemberton

I didn't much care for Tommy when I first met him. He was cute enough, certainly, a true blood bay Connemara/TB cross with a short-coupled body and a big eye. But too long the barn pet, he also, in my opinion, verged on the obnoxious—half class clown and half town bully. Whenever I took carrots to my own horse, Jury, stabled down the aisle, Tommy would bang his front feet insistently against the front of his stall, demanding his share. Annoyed at my refusal to give him all the carrots, he would let fly against the back wall—if he couldn't get more treats from me, he would at least bring his favorite groom on the run to admonish him, and perhaps slip him a peppermint.

I couldn't begin to understand why everyone doted so on Tommy, because, to my mind, he wasn't a very likeable horse. He had, for instance, little interest in people without food; if I approached his stall empty handed, he would turn away and studiously consider the spot where he wished some hay would materialize.

Simply put, the only reason I bought Tommy when Jury died was because he was there. Deeply depressed by the loss of a horse I adored, I knew that if I didn't purchase another one immediately I would quit riding altogether. I didn't bother looking for my dream horse, as that had been Jury, and he was gone. Anything would do, and Tommy was for sale.

"Don't even think about tacking him up in his stall," Stacy, the groom, warned me after I bought him. "He chews everything, including his wraps and blankets." We both gazed thoughtfully for a moment at the ragged Baker hanging on his door. "Try not to let him run over you in the barn aisle, but don't use a stud chain on his nose, or he'll rear. He doesn't stand well in the crossties, so have someone hold him whenever possible. Let's see, what else … oh, yeah, don't try to get him anywhere near the wash stall—if you have to rinse him off, just use a bucket and sponge. And make sure the water's warm; he hates cold water."

"Sounds like I should have had this one vetted for manners," I grumbled, only half kidding.

Stacy stared at me levelly for a moment, then reprimanded me in her flat New England drawl. "Let's be clear. The only reason you own Tommy is that I couldn't quite bring myself to hold up an ATM. He's the finest horse in this barn as far as I'm concerned, but Connemaras are slow to mature. He's still a baby, and he just needs a firm hand." She stared at me a moment longer, watching Tommy chew blissfully on the bill of my hard hat, then sighed, accurately gauging the likelihood of his receiving said firm hand from me.

But Tommy's ground manners weren't nearly as problematic as the issues I immediately encountered under saddle. In my haste to purchase him, I had managed to completely ignore the fact that he was only 5 and grass green, as well as that he was very uncomfortable for me to ride. His well-sprung rib cage offered a special challenge to my admittedly shortish legs, and he had no topline to speak of. He tended to be heavy on the forehand and practically impossible for me to balance; as a result, he tripped frequently, occasionally dumping me in the process. In addition, he was both sluggish and spooky, reluctant to canter but apt to kick out at a crop. And jumping was a nightmare.

Although I had owned "hunters" for some years, my career was so demanding that I had made only the spottiest of progress in jumping. Still, I could navigate small fences with some ease and had actually shown successfully in the Modified Adult Division on Jury the previous summer. But the first time I attempted to jump Tommy over a small vertical, I completely failed to anticipate the enthusiasm with which he rocked back for even the smallest of jumps and, as a result, I tumbled quietly over his shoulder. Everyone was surprised that I had come off, but no one more so than Tommy himself, who stood quietly on the far side of the fence and watched me with rounded eyes. "No one," he seemed to think, "has ever gotten off *there* before." And I continued to fall off virtually every time we attempted fences.

But as we worked together over the next months, Tommy began to change dramatically. He stopped spooking and began moving forward off my leg. He learned to gauge distances with the expertise of a school horse, ignoring entirely my own vaguely expressed instructions regarding pace and speed. He learned to choose the short distance rather than the longer one that usually jolted me out of the tack, and we were pretty certain that, somewhere along the line, he began to count strides. Even his flying changes were perfect and did not require a cue.

Most amazingly, though, from somewhere, he adopted the attitude and grace of a saint. No matter that I slammed down on his back and jolted his teeth with the (rubber) bit, his ears stayed forward and his manner serene. I could plant him so close to a wall that his hooves clicked against the base, and we would somehow make it to the other side. At the age of 5, Tommy had become a packer. My admittedly cynical view was that he was so embarrassed and chagrinned by my continual falling off that he decided to do everything in his power to keep me safe. A canny little horse, he no doubt realized that it had taken him years to find a mom, and he had developed a definite addiction to carrots on demand.

Despite the fact that names are very important to me, I had now owned Tommy for six months and couldn't yet order a stall plate. I had long accepted that his barn name would have to remain Tommy, as everyone in the stable thought it perfectly suited him, and I knew it would be impossible to get them to call him anything else. But his show name, Snappy Tom, surely had to go. "Think Irish, " I beseeched my fellow riders, and a list of names slowly grew. Daily I peppered my trainer and others with possibilities—Seamus and North of Boston, Publican and Phenom, Easter Rising and Aer Lingus … even, in a moment of weakness (or just poor taste), Sinn Fein. But none seemed right or special, and I threatened to call him Plain Wrap, as he still rather resembled nothing so much as an overgrown pony with a tendency toward obesity, a far cry from my fancy Jury.

The day of his final christening, we were riding outside, which both Tommy and I strongly preferred. My trainer had set up a simple line with miniscule verticals and called for us to trot in and canter out in five. Well, simple for some, one must assume, but not for me. As happened all too often, I thrust my body too far forward over the "in," causing Tommy to trip. He recovered immediately, but I was completely out of the saddle by then, with a death grip around his neck. Tommy jogged slowly to a complete stop and stood stoically waiting for me to sit back up. My trainer was practically rolling in the arena at this point, calling loudly for a camera. As stupid as I knew I looked, I could not get back in the saddle, and giggling myself, tried to figure how to gracefully fall from Tommy's neck.

"Sit up," my trainer hooted, "just sit up, you're killing me!"

"I can't," I yelled back. "I'm gonna hafta fall."

At exactly this moment, Tommy, no doubt tired of having all my weight on his neck, heaved his head up, thereby tossing me neatly back into the saddle; he then picked up the canter, jumped the second vertical and trotted proudly to the corner where my trainer stood. When he could finally talk again—he was now practically apoplectic—my trainer, wheezing with laughter, said, "Well, he's a keeper, huh?"

"He's apparently my keeper," I gasped back.

And Keeper he remains. ☙

Nancy Pemberton lives in Concord, Massachusetts with two border terriers and a contentious parrot. Her horses reside 50 miles away, in Essex; suffice it to say she has her reasons.

Saving Grace

By Kimberly Gatto

When it is dark enough, you can see the stars.

~Charles A. Beard

New Holland, Pennsylvania is a place of rolling fields and Amish villages. Tourists visit this quaint little town to purchase goods and view "the old way" of life. I made the nine hour journey there in search of something very different—one very special horse. This is the story of how I came to find her, in the most unusual of places.

I had been in the market for a young prospect after two unsuccessful attempts at breeding my mare, Chutney (whom I've owned for the past 15 years). Having recently turned to dressage after years in the hunter and equitation divisions, I was looking for a talented youngster that could take me up through the lower levels.

I was perusing the horse ads on the internet one evening when my trainer, Hilary Penlington (who is also a good friend of mine) sent me a message. She had found a website that I might be interested in, if I could stomach it. It was a feature on the New Holland Livestock Auction, which is held every Monday in rural Pennsylvania. The auction is a clearinghouse of "rejects," a place where old carriage horses, too-slow race horses, and outgrown children's ponies often end up being sold for meat—a world apart from the prestigious Keeneland Sale where Chutney had first been purchased as a foal. Tough as it was to view such suffering, people who knew what to look for at New Holland had been known to find some "diamonds in the rough." One such horse, Catch-22, had become an amazingly successful 3'6" hunter, winning good ribbons at Devon and at the indoor shows.

As I opened the website, I was not prepared for

what I was about to see. There were no photos of the gleaming coats and shiny hooves to which I had grown accustomed. Rather, the site was full of photos of thin, suffering animals, being trampled by others in the "kill pens," small corrals where the meat buyers put their purchases prior to transporting them off. Mares, stallions, geldings and foals were jam-packed together before being hauled away, many ill or injured, in double-decker trailers until they reached their final destination.

My stomach felt queasy. Did I want to do this? Could I handle it emotionally? As a show rider, I had never seen such unhealthy looking animals. I thought about Chutney and the many other horses I've known through the years. What if, by some cruel twist of fate, one of them had ended up at such a place? I thought about those sad-eyed horses all night, and when I finally was able to fall asleep, I dreamed about them. When I awoke in the morning, there were no decisions left to be made. I was going to find my dream horse right there at New Holland.

It was a crisp spring day when we arrived at the auction site. The horses were tied in rows to walls, pipes, anything that could hold a rope. Many were painfully thin. At the end of one row, a gelding kicked at his sides, obviously in pain from colic. Another had an obviously fractured leg. Many had sad eyes that told the tale of abuse. There were horses, mules, and ponies of all shapes and colors. All had auction numbers glued to their hips. Not a name, not an identity. Just a number.

Hilary and I walked back and forth, looking at legs and trying to avoid any eye contact with these poor animals. I first noticed a healthy-looking large bay mare, with a poorly braided mane and tail. There was something strange about her right hind leg. Nevertheless, I wrote her number down and continued on my journey. I kept thinking about the mare, probably because she was the healthiest looking of the bunch. I saw a few others that also looked decent; I wrote their numbers down as well.

As I weaved through the row of what looked like race rejects, a pencil-necked dark bay thoroughbred caught my eye. Her teeth showed that she was four years old; the racing plates on her feet proved that she'd just left the track. Hilary noted that the mare had good legs. She had a kind, frightened eye, like that of a doe. As her neighbors pinned their ears and nipped at her, the small mare nuzzled them back. I jotted down her number and continued down the row.

By now, some of the dealers had brought their horses into the small outdoor area to "show them off." As I looked on, a female dealer led the dark bay racer out of the barn. When the mare spooked at a booming tractor, the dealer screamed at the frightened animal. An old Amish man came from behind and pushed the mare's hindquarters. The dealer then grabbed the mare's halter, attached a bit to it, and, without a saddle, bridle, or helmet, hoisted herself onto the animal's back. Up and down the crowded walkway she trotted the dainty mare, whipping the horse's sides with the slack from the reins. I put a star next to her number on my sheet of paper. Any horse that would put up with such treatment would earn a star in my book.

By this time, the auction was underway. Having registered earlier, we took our seats in the stands. The first two animals led in were poverty cases. They went to the killers for $200 each. The auctioneer was shouting so fast that I didn't even realize that bidding was underway. Next to enter the ring was a chestnut gelding that I'd liked. He was announced as a registered Quarter Horse, five years old, with papers. Bidding began at $900 and rounded off at $1500, far too much for the killers to invest. Good for him. It appeared that he'd be going to a safe, happy home; all of these animals deserved such luck.

The next one brought into the chute was the dark bay thoroughbred that I'd liked so much. The announcer's words blared through the megaphone, "Four year old, just off the track." I turned to Hilary, "Should I bid?" I asked if she would do the actual bidding for me. I was just too nervous.

The bidding began at $200. The only bidders were the "killers" and me. We went back and forth. There was no way I was going to let them get this horse. When I went up to $460 (which, in the blaring sounds of the megaphone, we mistakenly thought was $640), they stopped bidding. The little mare was mine.

Emotions overwhelmed me as I looked at my new horse. She looked back at me with her sad eyes as I led her out of the auction area. It was as if she knew she had just been saved. And I had the perfect name for her. Despite her surroundings, this horse was pretty, dainty, and elegant, like Grace Kelly. She was Grace. Her show name was hand picked later on: Saving Grace.

The next few moments were a blur. What I do remember is that my emotions got the best of me as I led Grace towards the trailer for the journey home. As we weaved through the crowds, I was approached by a couple of seedy-looking dealers who offered to find me "the horse of my dreams." What they didn't realize was that I'd found just that in the skinny, frightened filly I now held close.

I was thankful that we'd be leaving now, before the "kill pens" would be filled with unwanted animals. My stomach churned as I caught a glimpse of the horrific-looking double-decker trailers outside in the lot. It broke my heart to think that, within hours, they'd be filled with helpless horses, heading for slaughterhouses near the Canadian border.

Grace traveled like a pro during the nine-hour journey to Massachusetts. Frightened, she had no interest in hay or water. Each time we stopped to check in on her, I saw fear and sadness in her eyes.

As darkness fell, we arrived home; I led Grace into her new stall. She'd be quarantined for a period of two weeks to ensure that she didn't have any transmissible illnesses. After that, she'd be free to begin her new life. She spent much of those weeks sleeping flat out, enjoying free choice hay, and gazing at her new surroundings.

I used this time to get to know Grace's likes and dislikes. She had no idea what apples and carrots were, and would raise her head high if I held them in front of her nose. While she had no interest in treats, I did find that she enjoyed having her neck and withers scratched. Nevertheless, she was always on edge, fearful of what I might do next.

Noticing the fear in her eyes, I decided to let her approach me whenever she deemed it safe. After scratching her on the withers, I often stood quietly in the corner of her stall, waiting for her to approach me. In time, she always did. As she began to trust me, she would walk over with less hesitation. Sometimes she would rest her head against my chest for a moment before ultimately backing away.

It was during this time that we discovered the probable reason why Grace had ended up at New Holland. As I discovered while researching her Jockey Club tattoo, out of 15 starts she had never won a single race.

The abuse that the little filly must have endured became painfully obvious when the farrier visited. She trembled from head to tail at the sight of his tools, and became agitated—rearing up, breaking things, and threatening her handlers—during the shoeing process. It has been a slow, steady journey to convince her that shoeing does not mean pain. With time and patience, she is making progress.

After a few weeks of rest and a clean bill of health, the moment of truth finally arrived; I was able to get on Gracie's back. Like any typical four-year-old racer, she had no understanding of leg pressure, hated going to the right, and had no concept of what a circle should be. Yet, despite several playful bucks, she was extremely willing and eager to please.

We have brought Grace along very slowly in her training; it is important to me that she does not become bored or frightened. She is a lovely, straight mover whose gaits are showing some signs of elegance as she learns how to carry herself. She is also quite athletic, as she demonstrates each day, romping in the paddock with her best pal, a 19-year-old medium pony. Grace is gifted with a buck so high that, while riding it, I am able to look down at the riding ring fence, which stands four feet high!

Like Hans Christian Andersen's "Ugly Duckling" (who became a swan), my scrawny, frightened filly has developed into a creature so lovely that onlookers often stop and comment on her beauty. With the build and fluidity of a prima ballerina, she truly is a pleasure to behold.

Now that she trusts me, Grace has developed a delightful little personality, similar to that of an impish young child. She expresses her displeasure by tapping her feet when she has to share her favorite cookies with Chutney, and becomes upset when her "paddock buddy" goes outside with another horse. She has clearly developed a sense of self-importance, which—given her background—I think is wonderful.

We haven't entered the dressage arena yet, but at five years old, there is plenty of time for that. This summer, I plan to bring her along to a few shows to get used to the hectic atmosphere before we actually compete. Hopefully, we'll make our debut at USDF Intro I by the end of the 2000 show season.

I once read a story that reminds me of Grace. In the story, one beautiful flower grows in a war-torn field laid waste to devastation. Grace is like that flower—a delicate creature whose beauty stood out in the midst of the surroundings at New Holland.

On a recent winter's day, the sun shone brightly and temperatures rose to spring-like degrees. Many of the horses took the opportunity to sun themselves outside in the paddocks. When I arrived at the barn, Grace was lying down—her long, dancer's legs tucked neatly beneath her, enjoying the warmth against her coat.

I walked gingerly toward her, and spoke to her in soft tones. I knew that many horses do not feel comfortable lying down when a human is nearby; it took years for me to build up that trust with Chutney.

Grace looked up at me with her soft doe eyes, but didn't move a muscle. There was no need to. Her eyes, no longer frightened or angry, now spoke of contentment and trust. As I approached her, she nuzzled me softly, and we basked together in the soft glow of the sun. ☼

As this book was going to press, Grace competed in her very first show, ridden by Hilary Penlington, and won both her dressage tests, USDF Intro 1 and 2.

Sojourner

By Rebecca Payson

Sojourner was one of those horses who deserved more than anyone ever could have given her, yet seemed to have gotten the worst of everything. No one knows where she came from, or started out. She was a miracle, and a disaster, and her memory springs thoughts of joy and tears of sadness. If she could speak, I am sure the horrors she would tell would be more than I can imagine. However, to me, her story starts in Ocala, Florida.

Sojourner came to me through my aunt, who was

working alongside a surgeon in Florida. The slaughter truck often came through her area, and a wonderful woman who owned a farm near the practice where my aunt worked would buy the best horses off the truck—the ones who appeared as though they might have a fighting chance at survival. She bought every one she could afford to. My aunt was at her farm one day when she saw some of the latest arrivals. Sojourner was one of them. She was filthy; merely bones and matted hair. But underneath she had a sweet eye, beautiful face, and impeccable conformation. My aunt bought the horse as soon as she knew the mare would live through the night.

This mare was 700 pounds underweight, had rain rot and crumbling feet. She had been everywhere, and no one knew where she had come from. She was aptly named Sojourner, for her travels and pains. Months later, I came down to see her. I rode her, and I fell in love. She was perfect. She was affectionate; she trusted me. Little did I know she would become my newest horse.

My birthday fell several months later, and I found out Sojourner was mine. She was being shipped up from Florida the next weekend. My mom, my best friend and I greeted her at Rockingham Park, a racetrack. She unloaded sweating, over a hundred pounds thinner than I had last seen her, and dehydrated. She had not fared well on the trip, but she was soon to come home and spend the best years of her life.

Within the next year, she relaxed at our farm. I rode her daily, and created an incredible friendship with her. She filled out, lost all her battle wounds, and became a big and beautiful thoroughbred mare. By the spring, almost two years after coming to our house, she and I were doing everything. She was incredible. I had finally found that special horse—the perfect one for me.

I started to ride her in Pony Club, and the first time she jumped, it was amazing. She had the form and style of a true hunter, and could move like one as well. We were thrilled. With each day, improvement seemed to flood in. She stopped spooking at things, and evidence of true training began to shine through.

Suddenly one day she was lame. We tried everything—medicines for every symptom, time off, and anything else our vets could imagine. Finally we took her to Tufts Veterinary School, where my aunt now worked. Sojourner had been lame going on six months. Nothing would relieve her pain, and no one could figure out why.

We had full x-rays done at Tufts and had some of the best vets available examine her. Finally, x-rays told us what we least wanted to hear. Her coffin bone had started to erode, and due to porous bones caused from her sufferings with malnutrition and neglect, there was a fracture.

The next morning, Sojourner had to be put to sleep. The damage had been done, and nothing could remove the pain. I remember the few hours before she was put down as if they were yesterday; I sat out on Tufts' grassy knoll, letting her graze, just sitting there crying my heart out. She had given me so much of herself. And she truly loved me back. Every ounce of trust and compassion flooded through her eyes to me in our last few minutes together. All I could say was how much I loved her, and how I didn't know how I would get through each day without her. When I kissed her goodbye she didn't pull back; she didn't do anything but look deep into my eyes. ♘

Rebecca Payson is 16 years old and has been riding all her life. She was born in Connecticut, but has spent most of her life in a small town in New Hampshire. Becca has had her first pony, Tag Along, from the beginning, and the collection has since grown to include several other equines. She enjoys writing, and this is her first publication. Becca currently shows in the hunter and jumper divisions, and has also taken part in Pony Club.

The Selling
of Stanley

By Judy Reene Singer

I bought him to resell him. That was the game plan.
I occasionally buy young Thoroughbreds from "The Shoe,"
an itinerant horse dealer with the unlikely name of Tom
MacCann, hence the nickname. He attends most of the
track and livestock auctions that take place anywhere from
Alabama to Massachusetts. The Shoe usually drives up and
down the Eastern Seaboard, making forays deep into the
South then up North again, selecting horses that he thinks
his clients would be interested in purchasing. And belying

his gruff, rough and ready exterior, The Shoe was even known to pull horses slated for slaughter off vans and adopt them out to good homes for nominal fees. We bought many nice young horses from The Shoe as well as a few clinkers that he grudgingly but always exchanged on his next time passing through our Long Island community.

My neighbor called me just before dawn one summer morning. "The Shoe is here with a truckload. Do you want to look at anything?" Asking me if I want to look at young horses is like asking a chocoholic if they would like to look at a box of Godiva chocolates. I was over to her barn with a fistful of cash before she hung up the phone.

The big six-horse stock trailer was crammed full of the usual menagerie: a miniature horse and miniature cow, bedded in straw and stuffed into an overhang; a small zebra and two llamas slated for a local petting zoo, knee deep in hay in the dressing room, and in the back of the trailer, two thin, frightened young geldings huddled together amid a sea of ponies.

"They had a bit of a rough trip," commented The Shoe. "We hit a storm on the turnpike last night and I slid off'r the road inter a culvert. All them ponies fell atom them geldings, so they're a little shook up." He turned the

Thoroughbreds loose in one paddock and the ponies in another.

I noticed the chestnut right away. He had a lot of chrome: white stockings, white blaze, solid legs and terrific conformation. He was only 3, The Shoe read from his notes, Louisiana-bred, papered, raced once and then hacked on trails for a few months. I watched as he moved with a light, elegant stride, despite two front legs swollen from being buried under 11 ponies. His hindquarters tracked deep under his body, and he carried himself with a certain élan. I watched him buck and stretch, trot and canter and liked the way he moved. I bought him.

Of course, the first thing he did, as did most of The Shoe's horses, was get sick. I kept him isolated in a back run-in shed while the poor creature fought off strangles, swollen legs, a banged-up eye and a bad case of hair fungus. In three weeks, with the help of my vet and a large wad of money, we had him healthy again. He had even managed to put on a few pounds, and the vet pronounced him able to start schooling.

Once I finally got on his back, I was disappointed to see he carried his head straight up.

"He rides like a giraffe," observed one of my students. "Why don't you call him Stanley?"

"Stanley?"

"Yeah, you know, after the giraffe who advertises Toys R Us. Stanley the giraffe." And the name stuck. Even after I learned it was Geoffrey the Giraffe, he remained Stanley, immensely flattering Stan my hay man who still, years later, reciprocated the compliment by bringing me the best cuts of hay.

The Real Stanley

To my pleasure, Stanley was a consummate gentleman. He rode quietly, was gentle to lead, stood for brushing, hosing, spraying, and clipping. He loved being groomed, and whenever my barn helper brushed him in her usual slow, meticulous way, he would go into a trance, closing his eyes and standing quietly. So quiet that one day she came into the house to ask me a question, accepted a cup of tea and chatted for two hours before she realized that Stanley had been left on the crossties. Accepting it with his usual magnanimity, he was napping when she raced back to retrieve him.

He was too quiet, I decided, and had the vet draw blood. It just wasn't normal for a 3-year-old Thoroughbred to stand around in his paddock and stare at his hooves all day, but his blood chemistry was fine. The vet surmised that perhaps Stanley had left some friends back in Louisiana and was just depressed. I put him on a program of TLC: extra attention, extra love and before long, his real personality emerged.

Stanley was now officially becoming a character.

He stripped the halter from any horse stupid enough to hang his head over his paddock fence, after which he would run off and toss it over the back fence onto a neighboring farm.

He loved to dig. He would stand for the better part of the day and dig an enormous hole until only his chestnut rump was visible above it. Then he looked for things to bury, like the lead left hanging by his paddock gate, or the big red ball I bought to keep him amused. He would carry things to his hole and bury them like a dog, painstakingly covering them up, then stand, innocently watching the ensuing frantic searches.

He fetched sticks. He knew how to unzip your jacket with the most delicate of touches. Shoelaces, too, got undone if you were talking in his presence.

He dunked his hay and his grain, turning his water

buckets into slimy lagoons. He dunked his brushes. Hammers and screwdrivers. Leg wraps and bridles. Everything went into his water bucket. Once, during a vet call, the unsuspecting vet left both a drawn inoculation and a lightweight spring jacket near Stanley's stall. Stanley dunked them with great dispatch and then offered the annoyed vet a slobbery kiss as he rolled up his sleeves to retrieve them. On more than one occasion, I had to help my barn worker look for her car keys/gloves/wool hat or sunglasses, only to find them you know where.

Weeks passed, and Stanley learned the basics of dressage very quickly. His neck relaxed and his head dropped down a bit. He carried his back up and tracked well underneath. He started developing a round, expressive canter and worked cavalletti with ease. Lateral work came naturally, and before long he was sailing through leg yields and shoulder-ins. I entertained the thought of keeping for myself instead of the usual training-and-selling routine, but my husband, to whom I promised we would reap great profits from Stanley's eventual sale, was always eagerly waiting for my progress reports at the dinner table.

"So how's that guy doing?" he would ask cheerfully. "Is he ready to be sold?" "Oh, yah! Umm ... you know ...

slowly," I would respond, guiltily enjoying my rides on Stanley more than I should have been.

Stanley longed quietly in side reins and learned square halts and counter canter. "He must be ready to sell by now?" my husband would inquire delicately. "Umm, slowly," I would respond.

A year passed. We decided to take Stanley to his first dressage show. I worried that he would be trouble to load due to his being smothered under 11 ponies the last time he trailered, but he loaded right up. And got a respectable score for a 4-year-old Thoroughbred at his first show.

"Great," enthused my husband. "He must r-rreally be ready to sell."

Okay, I had to admit it. He was. I put the ad in the newspaper. A very nice lady responded almost immediately. She was a policewoman, somewhat on the tall side, and was having trouble finding a nice big horse. Since Stanley had by now grown to 16.3 hands, her long legs fit him well. She was planning to do a little jumping, she told me, maybe some eventing. Since he was sensible about his environment, he would have been very suitable. We discussed his possible future with her while he stood on crossties behind

35

her. That's when I noticed that Stanley had learned to grin. His head was directly in back of the policewoman, out of her range of vision, so she couldn't see what I could see: Stanley's lips were spread apart, revealing big white horse teeth. He was holding his head cocked to the side and rolling his eyes around and around.

"So I'll come back with my trainer, and she'll try him out," the woman was saying, but I couldn't concentrate on her words. I was watching Stanley twist his lips all the way to one side, then the other. Then he opened his mouth wide and did the same thing with his tongue, waving it to the left, then to the right. Then he flapped his lips. "Trainer ... Saturday morning ... vet ..." I stood in mute fascination as Stanley produced the most amazing facial contortions I had ever seen on a horse, ending with the grand finale: with his ears flopped out to the sides like wings, he squeezed his eyes shut, raised his head and shot me a beautiful, heart-melting smile.

I couldn't bring myself to do it. I ended the discussion as diplomatically as possible and watched her drive away, while I wondered how I would break the news to my husband.

"Well?" he asked.

"She loved him," I said morosely and locked myself in my bedroom.

The First Sales

Two years passed and I still had Stanley. He grew broader and even more handsome. He learned haunches-in and simple changes and medium trot. I used him for my lesson students. I rode him and loved him. Everyone did. By now I had bought myself another warm-blood that I planned to compete. I didn't plan to compete Stanley because ... well, because he would be sold any minute now. In the meantime, Stanley was learning flying changes.

"I would like to buy Stanley." It was a phone call from one of my riding students. She had been riding with me for years and now it was time for her to buy her own horse. I had recommended she find something pretty enough to show, mannerly, sound and a good mover. We had been shopping forever, looking at videos, trying out horses that were none of the above.

I panicked for a minute when she called, and then thought: Hey. She lived locally, I would be able to visit him, and he would still be schooling with me. Why, it would be like hardly selling him at all.

She gave me a deposit and vetted him out. A week later she got admitted to vet school in Virginia and would not be able to take him. She canceled the sale. I returned the deposit and heaved a sigh of relief. I started Stanley on half-pass.

"I'm so-oo glad," another one of my students commiserated with me, then revealed that she too had been secretly in love with Stanley and was hoping to buy him herself as soon as she was able to sell her horse. She gave me a deposit and vetted him out. A month later she found herself in the middle of a bad divorce. She wouldn't be able to take him, she wailed to me over the phone, and canceled the sale. I gave her money back and Stanley an extra hug and figured we were meant to be together a little longer.

Stanley showed me a lovely pirouette at the walk that he figured out all by himself.

One summer I became ill and needed someone to ride my horses to keep them in shape. I met Lucy and Don at a riding clinic. They were from Ohio and living in Manhattan because of a job transfer. They were looking to catch-ride, and I observed happily that Lucy was a terrific equitation rider, soft, confident and curious to learn the basics of dressage. It was a match made in heaven. They came out to our farm on the weekends, her husband riding our resident paddock potato while Lucy rode Stanley. Then the husband would ride Stanley while I schooled Lucy on my Grand Prix schoolmaster.

Within two months they were smitten.

"I think we would like to buy Stanley," the husband approached me gingerly. "We'll keep him with you until we move back home."

"Well," I stammered, "I guess he is for sale." We negotiated a price. I was happy that Stanley had been sold to a loving, conscientious home, even if it was in Ohio.

They gave me a deposit. "Stanley is sold," I announced to all my students during our annual visit to the National Horse Show.

"Again?" they all exclaimed. It wasn't exactly breaking news.

Lucy and Don were going to take Stanley back with them in the spring, so I had the whole winter to get used to him being owned by someone else in another state.

"I'm proud of you," my husband patted me on the back.

Then one weekend Lucy came out from the city and took me aside. She looked downcast. She was being transferred to England instead of Ohio. It was a wonderful opportunity for her, and she didn't want to turn it down because of, because of ... a horse. I wrote her a check to return her deposit and after she left, I stayed there in the barn, staring thoughtfully at Stanley. He grinned at me over his stall and puckered up his lips for his daily kiss.

"I don't know what it is about you, Stanley," I sighed. He grabbed my checkbook and dunked it into his water bucket.

"I know," I said.

Still For Sale

"He's not sold?" Andrea, one of my working students, sounded delighted. "Then I'm buying him! I'll even keep him here in your barn! It's too perfect. I've been saving up and can't believe that I finally have enough and he's for sale again. It's just too perfect."

I didn't want to take her deposit. It was too nerve-wracking.

"Just pay for him when you're ready to buy him," I told her. "He isn't going anywhere."

The words were prophetic. After trying for six years, Andrea learned that she was three months pregnant with twins.

"Don't feel bad," I dismissed Andrea's apologies. "He knew."

Four months later, my husband and I sold our home and moved to the lower Hudson Valley in New York, to a wonderful house with a lot of land. It was perfect for us except it didn't have a barn. We would have to board out our six horses until spring when the ground would supposedly emerge from its snowy blanket and we could build a barn. The local boarding barn was very lovely, with heat lamps in the wash stalls, two indoor arenas and people showers next to the heated lounge. It was also very expensive.

"Do you think you could possibly lease out one or two of the horses?" my husband asked. "I mean, six horses ... board ..."

I found Barbara, a lovely woman who was looking for two horses to ride, maybe even possibly buy. She leased my Appaloosas and ... Stanley.

"Do you want to discuss price?" she asked.

"Don't be ridiculous," I brushed her off.

Not too long after, I got a phone call from Lucy and Don. They were back in the States and were hoping that Stanley was still available.

"Oh, yes," I replied wearily. "He's for sale. He'll always be for sale. That's one of the interesting things about him."

And I think I caught him winking at me.

Reprinted with the kind permission of **The Chronicle of the Horse**

Tom Tom

by Mary-Jo Anderson

The political tension in Dallas that late August afternoon was as heated as the balmy Texas air. The Dallas Police Department, and specifically the mounted unit, had been experiencing a tough couple of days due to conflicts surrounding the labor problems of Dallas teachers. Some crucial contract issues had not been resolved and the teachers were due to return to work. The officers on duty that afternoon were apprehensive, knowing that the tension they felt was not imagined.

Officer Darryl Crow and his equine partner, E.T., were exhausted and sore from the previous day's conflicts. E.T., short for "Exception to the Rule," was an 8-year-old thoroughbred who had joined the Dallas P.D. after a racing career in Oklahoma. Officer Crow had trained E.T. for police work, and the two were as devoted as any partners imaginable.

However, on this tense afternoon, E.T. had been removed from the duty roster due to his soreness from the previous day's action, which had involved assisting in the control of a rioting crowd at the school administration building. E.T. had performed admirably, but now needed some rest to ease his muscles and regain his strength.

Officer Crow would be riding Tom Tom on duty this evening. Tom Tom was a shiny, copper-colored sorrel quarter horse gelding who had been on active duty in the unit for two years. Before his police career, Tom Tom had been a show jumper.

At the time, the Dallas P.D.'s mounted unit numbered approximately 25. The human members of the department always had their eyes open for new "talent"— that special horse that caught their eye and had that extraordinary sense that can not be put into words, but is trainable into a valuable member of the elite unit. The horses come from all walks, but have one thing in common—they are well-trained professionals who are required, without a second's hesitation, to put their lives on the line for another's safety. The officers who worked with these horses on a daily basis knew instinctively what they needed in a partner, and it was no less loyalty than would be expected from another human officer.

On this afternoon, although Crow knew that the horses in the unit were as well trained and tested as any human police officer, he couldn't help but wonder how Tom Tom would react to him as a temporary partner. He thought about his usual mount, E.T., and reflected on the fact that he and Tom Tom had not had the years of bonding that he and E.T. had enjoyed. Would Tom Tom be as reliable as his usual partner and perform as trained, to the extent of sacrificing his own safety for that of his mounted officer, or even, in that rarest and most extreme of cases, lay down his life for his partner? Officer Crow had complete faith in the Dallas P.D.'s mounted unit, and put aside any doubts. There was no question that these horses were professionals.

A volatile crowd, comprised predominantly of students, was gathering near the front of the building, and police were in the process of closing down surrounding streets. Barricades were being set up, which served to heighten the crowd's volatility. The previous day's rioting had been dangerous and terrifying, but on this day, the police were better prepared. Although the tension that permeated the crowd of students had not abated, the police on this day knew better what to expect.

But the unexpected was exactly what was about to happen to Darryl Crow and his partner.

Tom Tom and his rider, along with several other police officers on horseback, calmly filed through a closed-off area for police and began heading down Washington Street, toward the Dallas Independent School District building on Ross Street. Their main duty was simply to calm the demonstrators and keep the peace.

Suddenly, the loud squealing of tires straining against pavement was heard simultaneously with the crash of a barricade being mowed down. As Crow and the others, both police and demonstrators alike, looked on in horror, a blue car lurched around the corner, tires screeching, fishtailing out of control. The teenage driver was speeding straight toward Tom Tom and Officer Crow.

The next couple of seconds seemed to be happening in slow motion for Crow; he now understood why, when faced with life-threatening situations, many people describe it as surreal and dream-like. What went through Crow's mind were all the doubts that he'd pushed aside earlier—how could he expect this virtual stranger, this horse who hardly knew him, to protect his rider above all else, now that they both were in true danger?

Crow attempted to steer Tom Tom off to the side, hoping that there would be an extra split-second for them to get out of the way, but, to his surprise, Tom Tom was facing the car down! The horse's training had prepared him to face down any danger so that his rider could protect himself. Tom Tom actually was putting Crow's safety above his own.

All Crow could do was brace himself for the hit. The 15-year-old driver slammed the car into Tom Tom with such force that the horse was thrown onto the car's hood and Crow onto the car's windshield. Luckily, Crow was not seriously hurt and rolled off the car when it came to a stop. However, Tom Tom was not as fortunate—the horse tumbled to the pavement. His leg had been caught in the front fender, which was causing him excruciating pain. It was a struggle for the horse to get up, trembling with pain the entire time, and limp across the street to a nearby lot.

Crow ran to assist the horse, but was limited in what he could do. There were dozens of slashes on Tom Tom's legs, and one of his rear legs was broken near the ankle. All the police officers could do was wrap the break, apply pressure, and get the horse to a veterinarian.

That evening, late into the night, ten veterinarians, assistants and anesthesiologists worked on Tom's Tom's cuts and bones to ensure that the healing would be as quick and comfortable as possible. Even with the help of physical therapists, Tom Tom was in agonizing pain for many months. Eventually, because of the horse's compensating for the injured leg, his good leg became inflamed and weak; soon it was causing Tom Tom almost as much pain as the injury itself.

Tom Tom fought valiantly to recover. At one point, he actually had become well enough to return to the police horse barn, and to begin working with his trainer again. The beautiful and noble horse was eager to please and seemed anxious to return to duty, following every command to walk, trot and canter, regardless of how sore and stiff he was.

But within a year, it was painfully obvious that Tom Tom, even on a modified schedule, could not maintain the stamina required for police work; his limp had become chronic. The police department retired him, and Tom Tom took up working with children as a rehabilitation horse. He bravely and patiently circled a track with kids riding him, day after day, week after week. It was as if the horse was intent on doing his civic duty, be it police work, community involvement or health care worker. Tom Tom seemed to want to help, unselfishly, in any manner.

But the lameness worsened, and Tom Tom could not hide his excruciating pain.

Tom Tom—one of the true heroes of the Dallas Police Department—was euthanized by veterinarians nearly six years after that horrifying scene one late summer afternoon in Dallas. The teenage driver who caused so much pain was sentenced to thousands of hours of community service.

It would appear that's the way Tom Tom might have wanted it. 🍎

Mary-Jo Anderson has been writing as a hobby since she was an 8-year-old with an active imagination. One of her first short stories as a child involved following a nickel throughout its life—passed from mint to bank, and hand to hand—and relating anecdotes of the people whose lives it touched. Living in the greater Boston area, she has followed careers in hotel management and public relations, and currently works as a proofreader/editor for a financial services company. This is her first published work.

The world is best viewed
through the ears of a horse.

Author Unknown

Oklahoma
Land Rush

By Lauren Schweppe

Last year, my horse Oklahoma Land Rush and I accomplished something I never would have expected—the AHSA National "Horse of the Year" title for the Small Junior Hunter (16-17) division. Oklahoma, or "Pipsqueak," as I call him, is the most amazing horse I will ever own, not only because of his talent, but because of the hurdles he has overcome.

It all began nearly eight years ago, when my former trainer, Trudy Glefke, went to a horse sale in Roswell, New

Mexico. Trudy earned her living through buying horses at these sales, taking them back to her farm in Albuquerque, training them for the show ring, and then selling them for a minimal profit. I had met Trudy when she was in Colorado, and followed her down to New Mexico.

While I had trained with her for only a year at this point in time, I had earned myself the distinction of "pony kid." Trudy would often get wild, untrained ponies in from everywhere, and I became the one nominated to tame them. It was a fun job for a ten year old, but a dangerous one at that. I would fall off, flip over, and/or get taken off with at least five times a day, but I was having the time of my life. And sometimes, when Trudy went to the horse sales, she'd let me come along.

Trudy always had an eye for a great horse; every person who has ever known her will tell you that. She could look into a horse's eye and see its potential. This is what happened when she came across a little bay gelding at the Roswell sale.

To me, the horse looked very sickly. I could see the scars from the strangles disease he had recently acquired, and I assumed that was why he was in the quarantine pen, way in the back. The poor animal was barely able to stand,

and was wobbling from lack of nourishment and dehydration. It was a nauseating sight.

Trudy walked right up to the horse. When he saw her coming, he shied away, showing obvious signs of abuse. Trudy took her time and eventually, the gelding let her touch his neck. When it was time for him to be sold, the dealers passed right by him, for Trudy had somehow found the owner and purchased the animal outright.

We arrived back home with only 11 horses this time, which was much better than our previous load of 32 (It was difficult finding blankets, stalls and pastures for all of those!). The new bay went straight to the front stall, and Trudy immediately called the vet for assistance. She had named her new purchase "Oklahoma," because that was the home state of the meat dealer who had owned him. Oklahoma was the fourth horse in the barn she had named after a state.

The next morning, I woke up, got dressed and went out to look at Oklahoma. He actually looked quite a bit better since Mario had clipped him. I went into his stall, and stood by the door, looking at the various cuts he had. You could see the stitches all over where the vet had mended his wounds. Oklahoma cowered in the back of the stall for a moment, then pricked his ears and cautiously made his way over to me. He leaned his head toward me to make sure I wasn't going to hurt him, then walked right over and let me smother him with calm, slow praises. Anything fast and he would jump. Mario had walked up and peeked though the bars, and I heard him laugh quietly at the sight of us.

It was a match made in heaven. Granted, it was not an easy job getting there. When we first attempted to ride him, Tomas got on him first, and came right back off just as quickly. Once we finally caught him, my trainer had me get on him. Once I was on and settled, Mario led him around in a circle. Everything was going fine until some trucker decided to honk at the horses. I was off within five seconds and got up just in time to see him clear the rail into the ring. Mario was quite certain the horse was to be mine then, but it took a bit of convincing of the parental units. My mom was great about the idea, but my dad wasn't too keen on it. Eventually he gave in and Oklahoma was mine.

I honestly never expected to come as far as we have together. We spent some time showing in New Mexico, Arizona and Colorado, and when I rode well, we won. There really wasn't much competition, and Trudy knew she had done all she could for Pipsqueak and me. Trudy then sent me to Florida to train with Bob Braswell and Christina Schlusemeyer. I had always read about them in magazines, but you can never imagine how stunned I was to find out I was actually going to be able to ride with them. This was a very big deal for me—to be able to train with somebody famous!

Since then, Pipsqueak and I have come a long way. He is thirteen now, and I am in the middle of my last junior year. He isn't afraid of people anymore, although he still gets a little nervous sometimes. You can still see all the scars from his past, but he's never gone lame on us, nor have we ever had any major problems with him. He's an amazing horse, and I would never have come as far as I have without him.

A couple of days ago, I was fortunate to ride Pipsqueak in the Small Juniors during the first week of the Tampa horse show. It had been exactly two months since my last show on him, because my sister, Courtney, acquired him for Christmas and had been doing the Children's divisions on him for the past couple of months. I had watched my sister on him all through Ocala with my heart aching because I missed being up in the saddle.

When I was finally able to show him again, I have

to admit I was very nervous. Once I got into the ring, however, something clicked. We won four of our five classes and were second in the other.

Pipsqueak and I totally understand each other. It hasn't always been easy; ours is a partnership that took eight years to build. And while I have other horses, this horse is truly special to me. Pipsqueak is like my child; I love him from the bottom of my heart. ♘

Lauren Schweppe is a successful junior hunter and equitation rider on the AHSA "A" circuit. Her recent accomplishments include winning the ASPCA Maclay mountain regionals and placing 2nd in the world equitation flat championship at the Capitol Challenge Horse Show. Lauren and her younger sister, Courtney, train with Christina Schlusemeyer at Quiet Hill Farm in Ocala, Florida.

Rhino

By Matthew Piccolo
As told to Kimberly Gatto

I often wonder to myself what kind of life Rhino had before he came to our barn. His eyes—the eyes of an old, wise soul—hold the secrets to an unknown past. The old scars on his legs may give some clues, but to what? Was Rhino the pony of a child who outgrew him, abandoning him for makeup and trips to the mall? Or was he a former camp pony who proved unruly and was left in a field? These questions often run through my mind. But while I may speculate until I'm blue in the face, Rhino—and only Rhino—holds the key to his past.

Rhino came into my life last year from the Animal Rescue League of Boston. He and three pasture-mates had been given up by an aging couple who could no longer care for their small band of horses. Rhino's three companions were all soon adopted, but the old-as-dirt grade pony was still in need of a permanent home. Luckily he found his saving grace in my trainer, who took him on as a replacement school horse for another aged pony who had recently passed away.

The aptly-named Rhino proved himself a project from the start. With a nimble buck and a will of his own, the 14.2 buckskin was talented at unseating his riders. It was pure coincidence that I outgrew my lovable 12.2 hand mount of four years at the same time that Rhino returned to service after a brief lay-up. And so began the challenge of my 14-year lifetime.

The first time I attempted to climb aboard the funny little horse, he cleverly attempted to drag me off the mounting block. I swung my leg over Rhino's woolly barrel and took up my reins. With nose pointed skyward, the little guy began to jig. Roughly two seconds into posting trot, he tossed in a huge crow hop. After a few good twists, and a blur of "SIT UP!!" from my trainer, I was tasting dirt, taking the bridle with me. As I attempted to catch my breath, my trainer and others had a fun time trying to catch the little rogue. Half-stunned, I laughed it off and hopped back on.

I was never one to give in to a challenge; then again, I had never ridden a horse like Rhino. My lovable medium pony mount was, for the most part, a willing and uncomplicated ride. But Rhino, like an old man, was set fast in his ways. He had apparently never worked that much in his early years, leaving him very limber and sprightly. He took to jumping with enthusiasm and excitement, once clearing a three-foot fence out of his paddock and into the middle of an ongoing dressage lesson. Rhino had little tolerance for rules; he'd long been doing things on *his* terms, and wasn't about to be "tamed" by me.

At first, I must admit that I let the old guy get the best of me. As I tacked him up, he'd walk around and ram me with his stocky neck. He liked being a bully, and was good at it too. What he didn't realize is that I, while less than half his age, was just as stubborn and iron-willed as he was.

While riding, I quickly learned to sink into the saddle and keep my leg on him. And to my surprise, I noticed myself really beginning to learn to ride him. Thinking ahead. Knowing that he's going to balk at the riding ring gate. Knowing that he wants to drag me over the undersized cross rail. Suddenly, I had to think not like myself, but like Rhino. I had never had to do that on any of the horses I'd ridden before. It was a new challenge, and I liked it. And while a couple of times I came out of the ring feeling horrible and embarrassed that I had let him "win," I had developed a renewed sense of determination.

Rhino and I have developed a relationship of give and take. He has already begun to make me into a more effective rider, and I, in return, give him the attention and patience that he most likely never had. This spring, we'll be competing at our first three-phase event, and I have no doubt that Rhino will teach me a lot about riding cross country!

And while I may never know the secrets to Rhino's past, I am certain of one thing. He and I have future together that is budding with promise. ♘

Matthew Piccolo is a junior rider who enjoys competing in local jumper classes and combined training events. After beginning riding lessons almost 7 years ago, Matt became immersed in his love for horses. In the fall of 1999, he began working with the strong-willed Rhino. The pair competed successfully in their first three-phase event this spring.

To Chutney
With Love

By Kimberly Gatto

Never shall I forget the time I've spent with you.
Please continue to be my friend,
as you will always find me yours.

~Ludwig Van Beethoven

There is an ancient proverb that advises us to "hold a true friend with both your hands." Centuries after that line was written, its advice still rings true. In our busy, chaotic world, a trusted friend is like a fine gem. I'm fortunate to have one such gem in my life—a beautiful mare by the name of Chutney.

In the beginning, Chutney and I were clearly a mismatched pair. I was a shy, insecure teenager; she was a fiery, opinionated mare. Having been diagnosed with scoliosis, I was forced to wear a back brace for three years—a clumsy apparatus that caused me to become the laughing stock of my high school class. It was not uncommon to hear kids ridiculing me as I walked by; some would even go so far as to "knock" on the brace. Needless to say, whatever self-esteem I did have plummeted.

Riding was meant to be my escape from such problems. I began the sport at the age of 13—a relatively "advanced" starting age, as I later found out. In the beginning, I rode at a small, backyard-type barn and competed in the friendly atmosphere of 4-H type shows. As I advanced, my pony and I moved to a large hunter and equitation barn where my lack of skills became apparent. I was a low intermediate at best, while the majority of my new stablemates were elegant equitation riders who had been involved in the sport since toddlerhood. Many competed regularly at Indoors and on the Florida circuit.

My trainer at the time had spotted Chutney while

searching for a 3'6" horse for one such student. While both he and the student were impressed with the mare's abilities, she didn't have the size or experience that this rider needed. My trainer, with the knowledge that I was quickly outgrowing my pony, thought that Chutney might be a good match for me.

My trainer never got on Chut's back, so he didn't realize that she was far too advanced for me at the time. The granddaughter of a racing legend, she had been purchased as a weanling at the prestigious Keeneland sale, and had been brought along steadily by a professional event rider. A "hot" horse, Chutney was used to a precise, accurate ride that would best showcase her talents and athleticism.

I fell in love with Chutney on the spot. She was stunning—a flashy blood bay with the most expressive, feminine face I'd ever seen and powerful yet floaty gaits. She jumped with her knees up to her nose and a round bascule that threw you right up out of the saddle. I liked the fact that she was a challenge. A true "diva," she'd pin her ears at any horse that passed by. And she wasn't about to put up with novice mistakes. If I asked her for a certain distance to a fence, she took it, right or wrong. Automatic lead changes? Out of the question. If I asked too roughly, she'd hop; if I didn't ask firmly enough, she'd fail to swap behind. This mare was a perfectionist, which was the one trait we shared (and still do, to this day!)

Perfectionism aside, we somehow complemented each other. Where I was weak, Chut was strong; where I was shy, she was bold. The memories of some of the jumps she carried me over still make me shudder. She may have thrown out a hop on the landing, or ground her teeth and swished her tail (big "no-no's" in the hunter ring), but she faithfully carried me over, day after day, year after year. In return, I trusted her with all my strength.

A couple of months into our partnership, Chutney became cast in her stall and suffered a serious—nearly career-ending—injury to her left stifle. The vet came immediately and stitched up the wound; however, dirt had already seeped into it and the leg subsequently became infected. At that point, the vets didn't know if she'd ever be able to be ridden again. I can still remember my reaction to that injury. As long as she was okay, riding and showing became unimportant to me; my mare's health and comfort were all that mattered. I stayed with her practically round the clock, soaking her leg and telling her how much she meant to me. Fortunately, with time and love, Chutney made a full recovery.

Showing Chut was a valued—though sometimes frustrating—learning experience. When I rode her the way she demanded to be ridden—relaxed, with a quiet leg, hand and seat, she could, and did, win with the best of them. If I made mistakes, however, she'd express her displeasure, which was usually enough to keep us out of the ribbons at the "A" shows. Our show results were based on how I rode on that particular day; thus, it was not uncommon for us to be champions one week, and come home empty-handed the next. These were great lessons beyond the show ring. Life, as we all know, is what you make of it; it's also a series of ups and downs.

While I often lamented the mistakes I made, I knew that I learned more about riding from Chutney than I would have had I ridden a more even-tempered horse. Sometimes I felt guilty, as if I were hindering her talent, but then I realized that she didn't care if we won a blue ribbon or none at all.

Chutney has taught me about determination, sheer hard work, and the power of believing in one's own abilities. I can vividly remember the time a well-known pro rider came to visit the barn where we boarded. At the time, I was riding with an extremely difficult trainer who told me that Chut and I would never be a suitable pair. When the pro rode Chutney, he agreed that she was a very "complicated" ride for an amateur. However, as soon as my trainer left the ring, the pro took me aside and whispered, "I really like this horse, you know. These other kids will learn to look pretty—you, however, will learn to RIDE." With his words of encouragement, I became even more determined to ride this horse well.

Chutney has been with me through all of the milestones in my life—first prom, SAT's, college acceptances, first car and when my first book was accepted for publication. Together we have celebrated victory, mourned rejection, laughed, loved and cried. When my father died of a heart attack when I was 18 years old, I once again found comfort by Chutney's side. And when the pressures of showing became too much, we'd often sneak across the street into an open field, where we galloped to our hearts' content.

I've always told Chutney the hopes and dreams that I've been too self-conscious to tell anyone else—one of which was to become a professional writer (a dream I'd had since I was five years old). I may never know whether she understands my words, but, like any good friend, she has a way of always encouraging me. Likewise, I hope that Chut has found comfort with me during the many times that she's been sick or lame. I think, in her own way, she knows how much she means to me.

It had long been my dream for Chutney to produce a foal. I somehow thought that by having her offspring, it might ease the pain of earthly parting when that dreaded day arrives. While Chutney was unable to carry a foal to term, I was fortunate to rescue Grace, another beautiful thoroughbred who becomes more and more like Chut each day. Thanks to the lessons that Chut has taught me, I've been able to do much of Grace's primary training myself.

Chutney and I know each other as well as any lifelong friends do. I know that she loves peppermints but won't give sugar cubes a second thought. I know that she'd give anything to stand outside during a rainstorm, and that when she curls her upper lip, it's a sign that she's not feeling well. And she knows that I sometimes take life—especially riding—a bit too seriously.

After 15 years together, my beloved mare continues to teach me. I recently took up dressage after years in the hunters and equitation. As we competed in our first Training Level test, I began to put the familiar pressure on myself. I tensed up, and Chutney, in typical fashion, reacted to it by throwing out a huge buck right in front of the judge's box. Years ago, I probably would have cried; now, sitting on the back of my 22-year-old friend, I could only laugh. It was as if Chutney, in all her wisdom, was saying to me, "It's only a show. Lighten up! It's our friendship that matters." Once again, she was right.

Together we have shared victories and disappointments; celebrated love and lamented loss; and have been there for each other through the proverbial thick and thin. And somewhere along the way, the shy, insecure teenager became a confident writer; and the novice rider became a capable and effective horsewoman. I'd be lying if I didn't credit much of that success to Chutney.

Regardless of whatever successes I've had, I sometimes get that familiar twinge of insecurity. On these occasions, I head straight to Chutney's stall and wrap my arms around her wonderful neck—and once again, I feel completely safe and secure. For Chutney is the type of friend that's worth holding onto—with both hands. ☺

You can tell a horse owner
by the interior of their car.
Boots, mud, pony nuts, straw, items
of tack and a screwed-up wax jacket
of incredible antiquity.

Helen Thompson, b. 1943

Your Horses Are on Fire

By Baron Tayler

Much as I love shoeing horses, my business interests have led me to design, patent and manufacture machinery for farmers who work with draft animals. Since the farmers and teamsters who use my machine work with draft animals almost exclusively, I acquired a few Percherons. They're the kindest, gentlest, most easygoing creatures on earth, but owning them created a problem for me.

I had only 10 acres of pasture; that's a little more than three acres a horse—hardly enough to feed three

1,800-pound horses year 'round without haying. Luckily, a nearby farmer has a large pasture that he hadn't used since he retired. I moseyed over and asked if I could use the pasture for the Percherons during the winter when I'd run out of grass. You should have seen his cataract-clouded eyes light up! He told me he'd just turned 91 years old and mourned the day he sold his last team and converted to tractors. Yes, he said, he'd love to have the horses in his pasture.

October rolled around, and the horses finally ate the last stalk of grass in their field. I walked them down the road and let them into the large pasture, which was knee deep in lush forage. They were in horsy heaven.

January arrived, and the horses had grown long, thick winter coats. The weather had been cold, but there was little in the way of snow. The field had a clump of trees in the middle and when it snowed, the horses snuggled up under a huge pine and slept.

With the first big snow came trouble. I was sitting at the breakfast table when the phone rang. It was a lady who lived in a house next to the pasture. She wanted to know if I owned the big horses. I told her that I did and asked her if there was something wrong. "The horses have no building to go into to get out of the snow," she said. I explained that they had the big trees to stand under, and that their dense coats were excellent insulators. I assured her that the horses were quite comfortable. Semi satisfied, she let me return to breakfast.

The following day the woman called back, and in a firm voice told me she was sure the horses were cold. I asked her how she knew this. "Because they look cold," she replied. "And, in what way do they look cold?" I countered. Silence. Not a word for 30 seconds. Finally, she said, "I just know they're cold!" "Okay, okay," I replied, "Why don't you meet me in the pasture in five minutes and, if the horses are cold, I'll take them into a barn." She agreed.

We met five minutes later. "Will they hurt me?" she asked. "Do they kick or bite?" It started to dawn on me that this woman was a busybody do-gooder who knew absolutely nothing about horses. With time on her hands, she probably decided that my horses needed rescuing and appointed herself their savior.

As soon as we entered the pasture, the horses trotted over looking for attention like three 1,800-pound "puppy dogs." After she watched me pet them for a few minutes, I asked her if they looked cold. "Well, no," she replied, "But it's hard to tell with all the hair."

"Why don't you put your hand on one and see if it feels cold to the touch?" I asked. It was obvious she had never touched a horse before.

Hesitantly, she reached out and touched one.

"Well," she said, "I have to admit that they do feel warm, but I still wish they had a barn to go into."

Just then one of the horses dropped a big, steaming pile of manure on the snow. She stood looking at it, quite puzzled. "What's wrong?" I asked.

No reply at first. Then she said, "Why isn't the horse standing in the pile?" "Why would he do that?" I asked.

"Because it would keep his feet warm," she replied. That snapped it! I was trying to talk logically with a certified nutcase! I left her standing in the field.

The snow melted a few days later, and I heard nothing more. Then another storm hit that promised to be a keeper. With the temperature staying well below freezing, I knew the snow wouldn't melt for a while, which meant I had to start feeding bales of hay until the snow was gone. Since my daytime schedule was hectic, I found it easier to feed at night, usually around midnight.

Two days after the snow had stopped falling, the old farmer called me. He said the woman was bothering him again, claiming the horses were not being fed. I assured him they were and told him of my nightly ritual. The local animal protection society called the next day, explaining they received a report that I was starving my horses. I invited one of their inspectors to come out and see for himself.

When the inspector arrived, I showed him the hay scattered over the field and explained my feeding schedule. I told him about the woman who believed horses should stand in their manure. I asked him to confirm my nightly feedings with a neighbor who had seen me feeding the horses. He did and was satisfied that the woman was, in his own words, a "Looney Toon."

A few weeks went by and along came another dusting of snow. The temperature hovered just around freezing, the snow melting as it hit the ground. The local animal control officer called. He was laughing so hard it was difficult to understand him. "Could I come over?" he asked.

Fifteen minutes later he arrived, still laughing. His face was as red as a beet! I thought he was going to have a coronary on the spot. Finally, calmed down to a mild chuckle, he told me that a woman had reported my horses were on fire!

The officer apologized for the inconvenience of his visit, but it was office policy to investigate each complaint. I was too busy laughing to even notice. Regaining control of myself, I climbed into the officer's truck, and off we went to check on my "roasting" horses.

When we arrived at the field, the sun was just starting to break through the clouds. Three gorgeous Percherons were standing there, contentedly munching on grass. Thick columns of steam rose off them as evaporated moisture in their coats condensed in the cold air. The officer and I were awed by the beauty of it, but soon the spell was broken. We both started chuckling again, almost rolling on the ground. "Your horses are on fire!" the officer roared.

I never heard from the animal control people again. However, the woman continued pestering the old farmer with a myriad of oddball complaints. I felt so sorry for him that I took the horses back to my place a month before I'd planned to. The farmer was sad to see them go. He still enjoys telling the story about those horses that were on fire. ♺

© Baron Tayler
Published in **ANVIL** *Magazine, August 1993*

Baron Tayler has been a farrier since 1976. He is a member of the American Farriers' Association, as well as a founding member of the Guild of Professional Farriers. Five years ago he started The Farrier & Hoofcare Resource Center, a web site devoted completely to farriery and hoofcare. The Resource Center has grown to be the largest equine-related web site in the world. Baron is available for seminars concerning farriery and the internet.

Son of Secretariat

By Tobi Taylor

In 1973, when I was 8 years old, I had my first bout of unrequited love. But unlike the other girls in my neighborhood, it wasn't with a teen idol like David Cassidy, Bobby Sherman or Donny Osmond. Instead, the object of my affection was a horse—Secretariat, racing's first Triple Crown winner in 25 years. I adorned my room with posters, spent my allowance on magazines sporting his familiar face and wrote a letter petitioning the Breyer molding company to cast a model in his image.

The decidedly horsy daughter of unhorsy parents, I had to make do for many years with a "dark bay or brown" Schwinn 10-speed, occasional rides on my cousins' grade horses and yearly trips to the Scottsdale All-Arabian Horse Show in Arizona. After my college graduation, I began taking riding lessons and bought my first horse.

By 1997, I'd ridden and owned a succession of horses for over nine years and was serving as a working student for Lois Whittington, a dressage rider, trainer, and "L" judge based at Flying Fox Farm in Scottsdale. One day, when former Swedish team member and Fédération Equestre Internationale (FEI) judge Christina Hermodsson was giving a clinic at the barn, Lois asked me to fill a recently canceled spot in the schedule. At the time, I didn't have a horse to ride, so after a quick check with the barn owner, Shelley Ebel, Lois instructed me to saddle up "Twinkie," a chestnut horse I'd barely noticed before.

I'm a bit wary of getting on horses I don't know, but Lois took pains to assure me that he—or rather, we—would be fine, that he was quiet and well trained. And, she added almost as an afterthought, "He's a son of Secretariat."

When I went to halter him, I looked him over thoroughly and felt sure she was either kidding around or testing my horse sense. This obviously aged, 15.3-hand gelding looked more like a big Thelwell pony, especially in his winter coat, than a son of Big Red. All he had in common with his so-called sire was his color and his markings.

But Twinkie's owner, Shelley Ebel, confirmed what Lois had told me. Not only was Twinkie—whose registered name is Statesman—a son of Secretariat, he was one of two colts that resulted from Secretariat's matings to non-Thoroughbred mares. I remembered reading that when Secretariat was retired to stud, after having been syndicated in 32 shares for a record $6.1 million, there was much speculation as to whether he could actually sire offspring. After all, Assault, the 1946 Triple Crown winner, had been practically sterile. *The Thoroughbred Record* had carried seemingly weekly reports for awhile about the status of the test mares bred to him, and the rest of the media were poised to call him a "dud at stud."

But luckily, Secretariat was able to get two out of three test mares in foal, and in late 1974, two colts were born. The first one, out of an Appaloosa mare, was a chestnut with a white blanket. He was later named First Secretary, registered as an Appaloosa and used as sire of Appaloosa racehorses. The second colt, out of a draft mare and also a chestnut, was acquired when he was nine months old by Don Montgomery of Ohio, who christened him Statesman.

As a youngster, Statesman's resemblance to his sire was striking. A magazine advertisement from the early 1980s notes that he was trained to Fourth Level in dressage. But he is known mainly as a breeding stallion and holds registration No. 000000001 in the American Performance Horse Registry. Bred to Thoroughbred mares, Statesman's offspring were larger, scopier and more talented than he was. Among Statesman's winning descendants are dressage performers Chief of State, State Trooper, Courier and Carbonero.

Unfortunately, interest in Statesman as a sire waned over the years, and at age 10 he was gelded, trained to jump and used briefly as a polo pony. Eventually he came into the possession of Shelley Ebel. She put him in training with Grand Prix rider and trainer Julie Sodowsky, who campaigned him successfully in dressage. A tendon injury incurred while jumping rendered him useful for only light work, such as the lesson I was about to have with Christina Hermodsson.

As we entered the dressage arena, one of the

Southwest's famous "dust devils" moved toward us, threatening to intersect our path, and bringing with it a flying, fluttering, white plastic bag. Just as we arrived at X, we entered the "eye" of the dust devil, and the plastic bag flapped underneath Statesman and through his legs. He didn't turn a hair, and I realized that whatever worries I'd had about riding this horse were unfounded. We went on to have a most productive lesson.

In late 1998, Shelly Ebel offered Statesman to me in an extended-lease agreement, and I gladly jumped at the chance to board him at my home in the desert north of Scottsdale. I hadn't ridden him since my lesson with Christina Hermodsson, and neither had anyone else. The first few months I kept him, we did little but walk the trails in the area. Periodically, I'd try trotting him, but he was quite lame in the leg with the tendon injury, and he'd drop hurriedly back to a walk, so I didn't rush him.

Gradually, though, with a daily massage, leg stretches and a lot of walking, he grew stronger, and we were able to do a few minutes of trotting during each ride. By March 1999, he was serviceably sound at the trot and canter, and as he grew fitter, I was amazed at the amount of suspension he still had. Just for fun, I began to play around at shoulder-in, haunches-in, half pass in trot and canter, and the occasional flying change—all movements I'd read about but rarely experienced. Just recently, with Lois's help, I asked for—and got—some steps of piaffe, which amazed and delighted me.

Statesman's time with me hasn't evolved into all work and no play, however. He shares a paddock with an Arabian mare one-third his age—jokingly referred to as his "trophy wife"—who bosses him around and helps to keep him fit. (She, incidentally, is a granddaughter of the chestnut Arabian, Orzel, known as the "Secretariat of Arabian racing.") Statesman has become the neighborhood mascot; children stop us on our outings to admire the "pretty red pony," and friends with fractious horses ask if I'll ride Statesman with them because he sets a good example.

At 25, Statesman will never see the show ring again, and even if he were perfectly sound, it is just as well—the caliber of horses in this country has improved dramatically since his heyday. But in my eyes, he is not only the scion of a noble line, he is the embodiment of a great dressage horse: well schooled, obedient, kind and willing. He is odd looking and yet regal, quiet but funny and affectionate. Most of all, he is very, very tolerant.

A few months ago, I spoke to his former owner, Don Montgomery, who said he always wondered whether Statesman had inherited Secretariat's enormous, 12-pound heart, the largest on record. I have no doubt that he has.

Reprinted with the kind permission of **Dressage Today**

Tobi Taylor divides her time between writing and riding in Scottsdale, Arizona. Her work has been published in American Indian Art, Archaeology, Dressage Today, Horse Illustrated *and other magazines. Aside from Statesman, she owns a thoroughbred gelding and an Arabian mare.*

"Ain't it the Truth!"

Author Unknown

A man and his horse were walking along a road. The man was enjoying the scenery, when it suddenly occurred to him that he was dead. He remembered dying, and that his faithful horse had been dead for many years. He wondered where the road was leading them.

After a while, they came to a high, white stone wall along one side of the road. It looked like fine marble. At the top of a long hill, it was broken by a tall arch that glowed in the sunlight. When he was standing before it, the traveler saw a magnificent gate in the arch made from mother of pearl, and the street that led to the gate made from pure gold. He and the horse walked toward the gate, and as he got closer, he saw a man at a desk to one side. When he was close enough, he called out, "Excuse me, where are we?"

"This is heaven, sir," the man answered.

"Wow! Would you happen to have some water? We have journeyed far," the traveler said.

"Of course, sir. Come right in, and I'll have some nice cold water brought right to you."

The man gestured, and the gate began to open.

"Can my friend," gesturing toward his horse, "come in, too?" the traveler asked.

"I'm sorry, sir, but we don't accept pets."

The traveler thought a moment, remembering all the years this horse remained loyal to him and then turned back toward the road and continued the way he had been going. After another long walk he came to a plain dirt road which led through a farm gate that looked as if it had never been closed. There was no fence. As he approached the gate, he saw a man inside, leaning against a tree and reading a book.

"Excuse me!" he called to the reader. "Do you have any water? We have traveled far."

"Yes, sure, there's a pump over there." The man pointed to a place that couldn't be seen from outside the gate. "Come on in and help yourself. There should be a bucket by the pump; your horse is welcome to share."

They went through the gate, and sure enough, there was an old-fashioned hand pump with a bucket beside it. The traveler filled the bucket and took a long drink himself, then he gave some to the horse. When they were full, he led the horse back toward the man who was standing by the tree waiting for them.

"What do you call this place?" the traveler asked.

"This is heaven," was the answer.

"Well, that's confusing," the traveler said. "The man down the road said that was heaven, too."

"Oh, you mean the place with the gold street and pearly gates? Nope. That's hell."

"Doesn't it make you angry, for them to use your name like that?"

"No," the man answered. "We're just happy that they screen out the folks who'd leave their best friends behind in exchange for material things." ☺

Even the greenest horse
has something to teach
the wisest rider.

Author Unknown

Silver Dawn

By Mickey Hopper

These days she looks more like a hairy marshmallow than a winning show horse. Time has swayed her back a little and shortened her stride a lot. Her right eye is hazy blue, and her mane can't decide which side it should lie on. But she has taught hundreds of children to ride, and brought back the confidence of a few adults as well. And if being loved means you live longer, she will continue on, well past her current 29 years of age.

Silver and I first met 14 years ago at a local hunter

show. Her young rider, Chelsea, managed to fall off in every class. The feisty Arabian/Quarter Horse cross mare seemed to think that she needed to complete a round of fences as quickly as possible. Often she would duck around one, sending her 12-year-old rider sailing over the fence without the horse. When their classes were over, Chelsea's mother came up to me and arranged for the child to have some lessons before the final show of the season.

In teaching the pair, I noticed that most of their problems could be traced to Chelsea's position, which was way too far forward. This rushed the mare, and then when a fence came up too quickly, Silver would just opt out. To this day, she won't do anything "the hard way."

Since we only had two weeks in which to prepare for the final show of the season, our lessons were spent working on Chelsea's upper body position and teaching her to relax. When show day arrived, she entered the show ring for her crossrail hunter class, and remembered to hum "Hickory Dickory Dock" to herself as we'd practiced, thereby keeping an even pace throughout the course. With a nice rhythm like that, Silver was willing to go over all the fences instead of her usual ducking out. This effort earned Chelsea a fourth-place ribbon, which she has to this day. It also established me as Chelsea's trainer for the remainder of her show career.

During their time together, Chelsea and Silver won many local championships. As it turned out, the mare was as talented at western pleasure as she was in the hunter classes. Yet as Chelsea's confidence grew, so did she. Soon her legs were too long for the little grey mare. When the youngster moved on to a larger gelding, her family decided to leave Silver with me to use as a school horse—truly a gift from God!

Every year since then, Silver has entered the walk-trot classes and won championship after championship. The faces of the riders often change, but the stocky little flea bitten gray mare is there, season after season. She isn't fancy, but she is steady. And it isn't just children that Silver has touched with her magic. She has taught many adults to ride, and in some cases, has helped them to regain the joy in their sport.

Wanda was an adult who decided that she wanted to pursue the childhood dream of owning a horse. She had only ridden a few times on rental horses, and now, at age 34, she was ready to begin learning the finer points of equitation.

After a few months of lessons, Wanda decided that she was interested in Competitive Trail Trials. Each trial involved completing a cross country ride of 20-25 miles within a set time limit, with the judges giving points for the horse's conditioning and his ability to handle the obstacles encountered along the trail. Wanda had her sights set on competing at the local event held near our barn in Antelope Valley. She knew that if any horse could help her achieve this goal, it would be Silver.

Wanda began to ride the necessary conditioning miles on the then 21-year old Silver. The only concession we made was to put shoes on her; it was the only time she didn't have bare feet. Wanda also body-clipped Silver in order to keep the mare from overheating under her usual woolly winter coat. When show day arrived, the novice rider on the old mare took fourth place overall for "best conditioned." Wanda has since gone on to her own horse, and does team penning now, but she still has that little trophy, proof that if you set your sights on a goal, you can achieve almost anything.

Cathy had a different problem. She was an experienced rider who had suffered a couple of serious falls within a period of a few months. One fall left her with a bruised heart muscle when the horse stepped squarely on her chest; the other planted her into an arena post and caused the fracture of several ribs. Cathy had lost her confidence, but was determined to return to riding.

Gradually and tentatively, Cathy returned to riding—on Silver. The mare's moderate height made riding seem less threatening, and her smooth and steady paces allowed even the most frightened rider to relax. Thanks to Silver, Cathy regained her confidence. While she has now returned to riding her own Arabian stallions, Cathy often brings her granddaughter out to our barn for rides on the gentle, patient Silver.

Silver's career as a school horse is bridging the generations, as Chelsea now comes out to visit her old friend, and brings her three little boys to ride around on the mare's broad back. They giggle and laugh as their mommy tells them stories about her childhood rides on Silver. And, of course, they bring handfuls of treats for the kind old mare. She may be a little stiff in the hock, and probably measures a little shorter than she used to, but her heart of gold shines as big and bright as ever. ☙

Mickey Hopper is the pen name of Monica Sellers. She is a dressage instructor in Lancaster, California at Sweetwater Ranch, a 30 horse facility. She currently competes at fourth level. As a writer, Mickey has had several poems published and is the author of the book, **American Eskimos**. She is also a song composer.

Toogie

By Mickey Hopper

It's hard to believe that Toogie and I have been partners for 20 years. I can still remember the first time I saw her, standing towards the back of a stall at the farm where I boarded my old gelding. I originally thought she was a three-year-old Thoroughbred and was surprised to learn that she was actually a five-year-old Appaloosa that had been given to my trainer. It was her second time as a "giveaway;" the previous owner, Sue Sally, had gotten her from a woman who had bought the mare as a weanling, and then just left her in a 24 foot square corral. Sue Sally obtained the young mare in exchange for a few riding lessons.

Initially, the pretty bay roan was so shy that she literally hid in her stall, just like a turtle in its shell. Thus her barn name "Tortuga"—Spanish for "Turtle"—or, Toogie for short. Her registered name was JustADream, but, at the time, she was more like a nightmare.

Sue Sally had tried to use Toogie as a lesson horse, but the mare kept bucking off the students. She had also failed as a polo pony, as she developed the bad habit of ducking whenever the rider swung the mallet. It was then that she wound up in my trainer's barn.

I began taking lessons on Toogie, as my old boy was long past the age of jumping. The mare epitomized the stubborn nature of the appaloosa—when she didn't want to do something, she could come up with a hundred evasions. What she hadn't taken into account was that I was even more stubborn than she was! I didn't know when to give up, and didn't have enough sense to be scared of her sudden whirls and bolts. And I'd noticed that she had a talent for jumping; she'd even jump the cross-country jumps when turned out in the field. I liked the little mare's courage, and respected her determination.

When my trainer decided to move to Texas, she had to sell Toogie. She kept telling me that I should buy the mare, but I was a college student with a shallow pocket-book. I could barely afford the horse I had; how was I to come up with any money to buy another? Fate suddenly stepped in, as I received a small inheritance from my grand-mother. And my older sister wanted to adopt my old geld-ing for use as a trail horse. So I spent my inheritance and bought the mare that no one else wanted.

Toogie and I had a wonderful career together. We evented through Training Level, and Toogie was always brave about managing on a budget. At the three-day trials, she would live tied to the trailer while I slept inside. When I came home from school, there weren't many eventing opportunities in the L.A. area, so I did jumpers, and then became really involved in dressage. We also did hundreds of miles on the trails. I always wondered if her blue left eye didn't see as well as the right, because she could spook with the best of them. I still have the stories to tell. There was the day when a deer appeared on in front of us, and Toogie spun around and headed back up the path at full speed, leaving her shoe behind! Or when we got stuck in quicksand, and the effort to heave herself out was so great that she popped five holes out in the billets of her girth.

At age 10, Toogie took time off to have a pretty filly, but it barely slowed her down. In fact, when she was nine months pregnant, we won a class at First Level at the LA chapter dressage show. During that pregnancy, Toogie bruised her eye and subsequently lost the sight in it. But it didn't affect her jumping, nor did it solve her spooking.

Eventually I began teaching full-time at my own barn, and Toogie was pressed into service as a school horse. While she no longer resorted to bucking students off, she would neither stop nor slow down for a rider who pulled on the reins and didn't use correct aids. She was an advanced rider's horse until I discovered the mechanical hackamore. This got the riders' hands out of her mouth, and, at the same time, gave them extra stopping power. It was then that Toogie came into her own as a school horse.

One of my students yearned to jump bigger fences, and listed "clear a four-foot jump" as one of her goals for the year. Toogie, then 22, carried her over that four-foot fence. Another girl, Lauren, wanted to compete in the Little Miss Rodeo contest. As part of this test, riders were required to perform a reining pattern complete with spins, slide stops and rollbacks. Toogie stepped up into the job. In fact, the mare learned to slide stop so well that more than once her rider flew right over her shoulder. Once Lauren learned to sit down, she could stay on and really make skid marks in the ring! Toogie also learned how to turn barrels and run the gymkhana patterns. Again, the little mare was so quick that, on one occasion, she left her rider behind on the first turn, and went on the finish the pattern before noticing that she was solo!

Now, at the age of 26, Toogie still works 5–10 lessons a week. She has finally slowed down a bit, and the ligament injury she had last year haunts her on cold days. Her roaning has spread; she is now almost fully grey. Her back requires special padding, as do her feet. But she can still manage a two-foot course and she will slide stop if you sit up and say, "whoa." And like her stablemate, Silver, she has a long list of youngsters that she has taught to ride. Toogie is usually the next "step up" as riders progress from Silver. At 15.1, she is a little taller, and has a larger stride. Toogie will alternate from English to Western simply with a change of bit.

Toogie's second and last colt was born when she was 21. He is half-Arabian, with a perfect blanket over a black bay body and just a hint of blue in his left eye. I am sure that he will carry on his mother's legacy of versatility, athleticism and the independent Appaloosa mind. The world could do worse than to have a few more horses like Toogie.

Toogie and Silver represent the precious tools of my trade. Without their cooperation, patience and love, I could never teach beginners to ride. They are a priceless pair, and I know that there is a stall lined with golden straw waiting for each one in heaven. I just hope they are willing to wait here on earth a little while longer. ☙

Prinz Eugen

By Max Gahwyler, MD

It was back in the mid 1960s when the manager of our club approached me with the news that he had "just the right horse" for me and that I should travel to North Carolina to see him. This horse was the brother of "Aldibelle," who was on her way to becoming the Horse of the Year, an honor that is no longer accorded.

The horse didn't cost much, which immediately made me suspicious. Knowing how many outstanding horse people lived in the Carolinas and Virginia, I wondered why nobody had bought this horse.

When I asked what he had done and what his problem was, I was told that he would no longer approach a jump; was panicky about the whip and being crosstied; could not hunt (and had almost killed a rider by falling into a ditch); often took off at lightning speed; and simply refused to canter.

I informed our manager that this horse's behavior spoke volumes about his trainer but didn't make it seem worthwhile for me to travel to North Carolina. He finally confessed that if I could not take the horse, they would have to put him down. He felt that this horse deserved a second chance, and that I could prove it. And so he decided to truck the horse to our club so that I might take a look at him.

The horse was absolutely beautiful. At the time, we had three friends as guests: Maj. Wikne, Col. Hans Handler and Bill Steinkraus; all agreed that this was a great horse to look at, but riding was another matter. I felt sorry for the horse, nicknamed "Headlight" for his long blaze, and since we had an empty stall, I put him in it for a few days (or so I thought). Never did it occur to me that he would still be there today—nearly 34 years later. We also changed his name to Prinz Eugen as a symbolic nod to his past.

My education of this horse was a total failure. One year later, I was still unable to canter him. I had been thrown out of the arena, into the bleachers and over the outdoor fence. When he saw polo matches with riders swinging mallets, he shivered; and he never went close to even the lowest hunter fence, particularly when painted.

The real education—or rehabilitation—was not completed by me or any other experienced rider, but rather, by my wife's experienced hunter, Gray Lady, a.k.a. Gracie. Gracie was level-headed, totally safe, reliable and of undetermined origin. She had found us in Vermont in 1960, at a cost of $150. There was never any question that she was the boss of all our horses and always "number one" in the hunt field, but never ahead of the huntmaster. She thought very little of dressage, but anything else was great!

Every spring, our horses went to the farm in Vermont for a relaxing time of trail riding, swimming and no real hard work. They had acres of open land and woods, and total freedom to come and go in the large fenced-in area. When we wanted them to come in, we blew a whistle, and led by Gracie they would come to the barn for feeding. Having never been in a position like this, Prinz simply followed Gracie and the pony, "Dukie Gumdrops."

After a few weeks, we saddled up and simply on a loose rein, Prinz followed Gracie in walk, trot and canter. To my amazement, we jumped over logs and stone walls. He learned to go down steep slides and follow narrow trails and eventually he learned to swim in our lake.

Back home in the fall, Prinz was a totally transformed horse. We began basic work in the polo field until I had exactly what I wanted. We then transferred our accomplishments into the dressage ring; however, I never corrected or schooled him in this setting. Prinz thus realized that coming down centerline was fun. Soon, his real character as a "show-off" came to be recognized. Approaching the ring, he just puffed up and had a fabulous presence and forwardness, which he maintained throughout his showing career from Training through the FEI levels.

Even today, at the ripe old age of 38, he still puffs himself up going down centerline, doing his lateral work in trot, and flying changes at canter. And I, as in the past, just sit there smoking my pipe and thank my fate for having given a horse like Prinz a second chance and giving me a friend for life. Together we are probably the oldest team in the USDF Century club, still riding every day, full of enthusiasm and trust.

Max Gahwyler, MD, and his wife Doris came to the U.S. from Switzerland in 1952. Their interest in horsemanship has been shared for over 40 years of marriage. It was through their friendship with the late Col. Hans Handler of the Spanish Riding School in Vienna that the Gahwylers became interested in dressage and convinced of its value as a foundation for all good riding.

Dr. Gahwyler played a major role in the development and promotion of dressage in the U.S., including a stint as president of the American Dressage Institute, the forerunner of the USDF.

An AHSA "S" judge, Dr. Gahwyler is also a popular clinician with a special interest in teaching and promoting sound basics in dressage. Dr. and Mrs. Gahwyler live in Darien, Connecticut.

Sundown

By Rachel Farris

Sundown wasn't the horse of my dreams. To be frank, he wasn't even close. But he was my horse, and mine alone. The fall I was in fifth grade, I was flipping through the classified ads, and my eyes became fixed on one such ad. The first words of the ad read, "Hunter/Jumper Prospect," indicating a horse that can be trained in the English riding style of hunting and jumping, which is how I'd learned to ride. I became excited about this particular horse, advertised as, "Welsh pony, very sweet. Call for details."

I'd been riding horses since I was five years old, but

for the last several years, whenever I'd asked my parents about purchasing one for me, they'd refused. Yet, after reading the classifieds on this day, I asked my dad about buying a horse and hinted how cute a pony would be. To my shock and joyful surprise, he said, "Want to call them?"

I quickly nodded. This was the first time in history my dad had actually said, "Let's call them!" about a horse. I couldn't wait to find out what this pony would be like. I imagined a well-tended stable with a riding arena and a nice instructor who would let me jump, canter and try out the horse of my dreams.

Soon enough, we were headed out in my dad's truck, with me squeezed between him and Robin, a horse-owner friend of the family who boarded at a nearby stable. As I was currently unhappy with my instructor and stable, I had high hopes that owning a horse would give me the satisfaction I was looking for.

I knew it was almost impossible to think that my parents would ever be able to afford a horse at the stable where I rode. But I thought that maybe I could keep the pony where he currently stayed, or perhaps at Robin's small barn. I simply wanted to own a horse or pony—Anything I could ride.

We arrived at the stable and my bubble burst. The mouse brown-colored bay pony, which the man explained was a "little off" in the back hind leg, was dead lame. The stable owner had a Western saddle on the tiny pony. He wasn't exactly the type of horse a girl who rides English would want. As I viewed about 15 horses in the paddock, I realized that the man must run a place where people could rent horses and go on trail rides.

I'd always wanted a palomino, and so did my dad, even though they aren't common in the hunter ring. I thought palominos were beautiful. When the man, who saw we were obviously disappointed in the pony, approached us, my dad asked about the rest of the horses. The old man's eyes lit up as he pointed to the prettiest ones: a beautiful black and white paint and a well-built Morgan.

"Y'all," he said, in a rough Texas accent, "can have anyone but them two!"

Then I saw the palomino. "That one, Dad!" I said.

The man looked over at the palomino. "Ah, yeah, Trigger?" He immediately began working, moving the rest of the horses into a corral. The owner kept pointing to a furry brown horse with the letters "JD" on his shoulder, which was probably the brand for the ranch. The man had named the horse JD. Original. He'd named the mouse-brown pony Mouse, and the Morgan horse Morgan.

I pushed JD aside and firmly stated that I wanted to ride Trigger. As soon as I started riding the Quarter Horse around the paddock, I was already thinking of names for him. When I asked Trigger to canter, he'd go for about five strides and stop in front of his owner. Because of his behavior, I thought that he was too loyal to this owner and would be very, very difficult to train. I found out later that Trigger had stopped because he was so hungry, and he knew that this was the man who fed him.

When we went home, I kept talking about Trigger. My mother was opposed to my getting him. He wasn't too expensive, but she didn't understand why I needed a horse if I could just take lessons. While we were walking around the neighborhood one evening, I kept trying to convince her that I should have a horse. All the while, I was thinking of names for Trigger. Finally, my mom said that I could get him. Since it was around sundown, I decided to call the horse Sundown Walker, or Sundown for short.

Sundown turned out to be difficult to train. He'd been working as a trail-riding horse and was used to being asked to do things by beginner riders who couldn't control him. But when I rode him, Sundown had a very smooth trot. His mane was a beautiful creamy white and his coat shone light golden. He had a flood of white hairs in a beautiful blaze going down his face. His socks were always clean with no grass stains to see. I grew to love him with all of my heart.

When we first got Sundown as a seven-year-old, he was quite skinny. He'd obviously been underfed and undernourished. But he worked up to a large bucket of sweet feed a day and slowly got back into shape.

I remember I used to go out into the pasture while Sundown ate. I'd sit and sing to him the first song that came to mind—from "Daddy's gonna buy you a mockingbird" or a new country song. I'm a terrible singer, but Sundown never minded. He'd just put his head in my hands and sort of sigh a little. I remember that I sang one song, "With a Broken Wing," because it's about someone who's been hurt and is doing well now even after being abused. There's a line in it that says, "You ought to see her fly." That song reminded me so much of Sundown. He was recovering from his previous rough life, and, together, we were learning to fly.

I ended up boarding Sundown at Robin's barn. As it turned out, the barn manager was extremely helpful. She'd hold Sundown while the farrier worked with him. Sundown was deathly afraid of getting new shoes and he'd tremble and shake. But he was dearly sweet in the pasture when he was roaming around, and even as I rode him.

I also suspected that Sundown feared men because the only man he'd let near him was my dad. I think that's because Sundown knew Dad was the one who had bought him for me.

Sundown and I never got to show—something I used to think was very important. We never got to jump. We never got to do flying lead changes. We never got to do so many things. One night in March, before he turned eight years old, Sundown broke his leg while frolicking in the pasture. He had to be put down. This horse hadn't been with me for more than six or seven months, but his death hurt me so much that I stopped riding for nearly a year.

Eventually, my broken heart healed enough for me to begin riding a seven-year-old Thoroughbred named Ricky, who is sweet and beautiful. Because Ricky is hardly trained, many people ask me what I see in him. I just smile to myself as I recall the great lessons Sundown taught me.

Sundown showed me what the important qualities are in a horse, or in anybody. He helped me to see that kindness and a good heart are much more valuable than how perfectly trained or well-bred a creature might be. With his devotion, he taught me how to love unconditionally. Ricky is special himself, but I also love him because he brings back memories of happy times with Sundown. Ricky and I ride once or twice a week. Somehow, I think Sundown would approve.

I know that Sundown is in heaven watching over me when I ride. I take falls, but I'm never more than bruised, and the only thing broken is my pride.

Instead of being the horse of my dreams, Sundown has become the horse in my dreams, where we do things we couldn't accomplish during his life. In my dreams, Sundown is never hungry or in pain. He brings back memories of our good times in the pasture, of the first time we cantered, or the day that I went out to the barn and could not see his ribs anymore.

In my dreams, Sundown and I jump; we soar.

You ought to see us fly. ☙

Rachel Farris, 16, lives in Austin, Texas. She has loved horses since she was five years old. Her other passion is writing. Rachel gratefully credits her eighth grade English teacher, Ms. Wendy North, for inspiring her as well as being a wonderful mentor. "Not only is she an amazing teacher of the English language, but she is a heartwarming woman who is extremely kindhearted and positive." Rachel currently rides with Beverly Monroe, who "is the best trainer I've ever ridden with. She makes me love horses even more than ever, which I never thought possible."

Commanche Cloud

By Lisa Parker

He was born in May of 1963. His mother was a small registered Quarter Horse mare; his father was a traveling rogue who kept his dalliance discreet. From this pairing was born a steel blue boy with a blaze and three stockings. This fluffy gray baby, who resembled a spring storm cloud, came into the world at a time when the Disney film Commanche the Horse was popular. The little lad was thus named Commanche Cloud.

He was taught to work harness as a yearling with

the hope that he'd one day become a draft pony, but, spotted by a local horseman, he was destined for greater things. He was registered as a Quarter Pony with the registry number of 73.

Commanche went on to become four-time West Virginia 4-H state champion in both pony trail and western pleasure. He was five-time Ohio State 4-H champion trail and pleasure pony. At the age of 26, he made his final appearance at the Ohio State Fair, bringing home the blue ribbon in pony hunter under saddle. Commanche accomplished these feats with six different young riders, three of whom are now professional horsemen.

Commanche not only taught and "babysat" riders, but other horses as well. The first "baby" he raised was Castor Creek ("Cass"). Twenty-five years later, after she had become blind, he would also save her life.

It had been raining steadily for several days. On the night of March 1, 1997, the floodwaters quickly began rising in our lower paddock. By 2:30am, the situation had become dangerous. We knew we had to get the horses to safety.

The floods had knocked our electricity out, so there was no light except for the glow of our flashlights. Holding onto the fence in the darkness, my husband and I called each of the horses over, one by one. He knocked down a portion of the fence so we could pass through, as I climbed onto their backs and swam each one, separately, to drier land. As the waters continued to rise, we had rescued all but two of the horses: our blind 25-year-old mare, Cass, and her constant companion, Commanche Cloud.

Something had to be done soon. As the storm gained momentum, the field was a raging torrent. The water was already chest-high on the horses. As we called to the horses, Commanche came to our voices and to safety, but the loud rushing water confused the blind Cass. She remained chest-high in water, flailing about in the angry tide.

In a desperate effort, I climbed onto 34-year-old Commanche's back. The brave little pony summoned his might and swam through the deep, muddy waters towards his companion. When we reached the mare, I clipped a lead onto her halter, and she swam back with us. Thanks to Commanche, Cass had found safety.

After arriving on dry land, we turned all of the horses loose in the upper fields to find their own safety. The next morning, we awoke to find Commanche watching over and protecting his blind companion. He had never left her alone.

The following February, at the ripe old age of 35, this wonderful old grump who had taught so many, found his way to greener pastures.

We still miss Commanche Cloud, World's Greatest Pony. 🍎

Lisa Parker's love of horses began when she was a child. Her mother, Sam Miller, became involved with horses as a family activity 30 years ago, being a single parent with Lisa and her brother. Lisa and her husband, Calvin (also a life-long horse owner), have owned and operated Second Chance Farm near Chillicothe, Ohio for 16 years. They raise, train and show Quarter Horses, a passion they have passed on to their son, Jonathan. Second Chance Farm has three horses over the age of 25, one of whom gave birth (at 26) in the spring of 2000!

To be loved by a horse,
or by any animal,
should fill us with awe,
for we have not deserved it.

Marion C. Garretty

Big Ben:
Remembering an
Old Friend andTeacher

By Staci Hill

It's 11:58 pm and I'm writing this article because I'm unable to sleep. Approximately two hours ago I received some of the most heartbreaking news I've ever received—Big Ben died on December 11.

My grief and tears are shared by many across the equestrian world, but in my case it's different. For five years it was my great honor and pleasure to be Big Ben's main groom and caretaker.

I now reside in Brentwood, Tenn., just outside of

Nashville, where I'm employed at Brass Lantern Farm. Prior to this, I lived in Perth, Ontario, at Millar Brooke Farm, home of the great Ian Millar and, of course, Big Ben.

After approximately eight months of employment at Millar Brooke, Big Ben became one of my main responsibilities. All of the grooms at the farm played an active role in caring for Ben, but he was under my care since I was the home groom. While the other grooms went to many shows, I would stay at Millar Brooke and care for the farm, the horses who stayed home, and most importantly, Big Ben.

I rode Ben almost every day, stretching him out and helping him keep a healthy degree of fitness, while at the same time keeping in mind that he was retired and didn't need to work. When I went to Millar Brooke I knew I could ride, but I didn't expect to ride in the company I was keeping. It wasn't uncommon to be hacking around the ring with Jill Henselwood, Gail Greenough and Ian. In normal circumstances, people with such experience and horsemanship would have intimidated me. But it was OK because I was aboard Ben.

Looking back, I don't ever think I got over the awe of him. Maybe it was because I was an American who had been placed in a position to care for one of Canada's legends. And if anything went wrong … let's just say that the thought is not a pretty one!

Maybe part of the awe came from the tours of people that ranged from all ages, races and walks of life who would make the trip to Millar Brooke. Sometimes they would travel from halfway around the world just to meet this magnificent horse. It may have been that he had a heart bigger than Canada itself. No matter how he felt—whether good or bad—he never gave less than 150 percent and never asked for anything in return.

I loved every minute of caring for him. Through all the good times and a few bad times, through sickness and good health, I wouldn't trade a second of it for $1 million.

The Morning Routine

The world knew Ben as a competitor, but I knew him on a different level. When Ben was in the competition world, I would watch and cheer for him every time he and Ian entered the ring. Not unlike a majority of the population, I knew him only through TV.

I met Ben during his retirement tour. The first and only show where I saw him was his retirement ceremony at the Royal Winter Fair in Toronto. It was the first time I'd witnessed Big Ben in front of his countrymen and fans. That experience is one I won't forget. Even though Ben was officially retired, he was always a competitor.

I will always cherish the memories of Ben. Every morning when I turned on the lights in the barn, the first thing I did was open his door and attach his stall gate so he could hang his head out. It was one of Big Ben's rules. Then, I became a human scratching post. In most instances it's a terrible habit to let a horse scratch on you, but Ben had more than earned that privilege.

Once Ben was done scratching his head, he had a special spot, just at the top of his withers, that had to be scratched as well. If any part of this regimen was missed, or not done to his standards, I was either ignored for the rest of the day or I had to deal with a temperamental attitude.

For example, Ben had a big, beautiful double stall with a window at one end and an open door with a stall guard at the other. If he felt I hadn't done an adequate job in scratching him, I could count on one of two things happening while cleaning his stall: (a) he would walk in front of me and stop with his shoulder right in my face; or (b) he would walk up behind me, put his chest to my back, then place his head over mine so all I could see was his massive jaw. He would stand there until I scratched him.

If I didn't respond in the appropriate manner, he would gently "body tap" me until I did. It was all done in good humor, and it was a fun game for both of us. He would always make me smile, even if I was in a big hurry to get done.

Ben's wants were so simple and easy it was almost mind-boggling. This was an animal who had traveled and seen more than most people will ever see in their lifetimes, yet his favorite place to hack was on a quarter-mile oval track that was alongside Millar Brooke's lane. Each time we went to this track, Ben would put his head up, prick his ears forward, and act like he was 5 years old again. He would sometimes become bigger than life.

When he was in a feisty mood, he would prance, snort, spin and do anything to catch me off-guard—and, believe me, at 23 years this old-timer still had that spark. Other days, if he was in a tranquil mood, I could ride him with a loose rein and he would walk calmly and breathe deeply as if he were just enjoying the moment.

Extra-Special Moments

As I've already mentioned, Ben received many visitors from all over the world, and it was my honor to greet these loyal fans and introduce them to him.

There was a young boy, I believe he was 11 or 12, and we granted him, his aunt and uncle (who happened to live just a few miles down the road) and a couple of other relatives a special private tour. Now, granting private tours wasn't uncommon, but this particular instance had several special twists.

First, this young boy had severe physical challenges. He was in a wheelchair and didn't have control over his bodily functions, yet mentally this boy was a genius. His only medium of communication was through a board with letters, symbols and numbers. He would point and spell out what he wanted to say.

Ben and Ian were the biggest heroes in this boy's life. So when his aunt and uncle learned their nephew and his family were coming to visit, they asked if they could set up this special meeting.

When they drove down the lane, the boy noticed the farm sign and became excited. His family said they were just going to look at the farm but didn't think Ben was there. When they arrived, I brought them to the indoor arena.

Next, I brought out a couple of the other horses for

him to see, but I could tell by his actions that he was really hoping to see Ben. When I finally walked out with Big Ben, the boy's reaction was unforgettable. He was so elated he couldn't control himself or his emotions. His arms started moving in erratic motions, he started crying loudly, and his legs were banging on the wheelchair. Most horses would have turned and bolted from the situation. But not Ben.

I'd been holding Ben on a loose shank. He not only approached the boy, but he also put his head to the boy's face as if to give him a kiss and tell him that it was OK. Ben not only made this sweet gesture, he continued to keep his head near the boy so he could pet him.

There wasn't a dry eye in the house. It was the first time in my life that I'd witnessed such professionalism and horsemanship—and I learned it from a horse, not a human.

Several other children from the Make-A-Wish Foundation also visited Ben. Their last wish was to see the great horse. On many occasions, if it was at all achievable in a safe manner, Ian and Ben would surprise the child with a ride. Each of these tours was a memory in itself. In all of the visits and rides, Ben never once took a misstep that may have put a child in danger. It was almost as if he knew that there was someone very special sitting on his back.

Ben entertained hundreds of visitors a year and will always be remembered as one of the greatest ambassadors of the equine sport.

I want to thank Ben for being my greatest teacher— not only in the aspect of becoming a better rider, but also teaching me how to become a good horseman.

I will miss his morning nickers when I enter the barn. I will miss seeing him trot across the grass paddock with his head held high and his tail in the air. But I think the thing I will miss most of all is putting my arms around his neck and giving him his favorite double-wither scratch.

Finally, my biggest thanks of all is to Ben for allowing me to touch my dream. Many riders, not unlike myself, dream of making it to the Grand Prix level and competing on a good horse. If for some reason I don't reach my dream, I will never regret any of my life's efforts.

Thanks to you, Ben, at least I know what it was like to ride, care and, most of all, love one of the greatest horses of all time. ♘

Reprinted with the kind permission of **The Chronicle of the Horse.**

Farley and MoAlla:
A Love Story

By Cooky McClung

Farley was strictly a horse cat. As working felines go, he was no great shakes in the barn. He loved being there, but wasn't any too keen on joining in with the chores. Obviously, Farley's job description didn't include nabbing mice before they invaded the feed room or chewed on tack. It didn't cover chasing vermin out of the hayloft or preventing them from sneaking about the feed tubs to clean up leftovers.

Unlike his four aloof cohorts, this cat had formed an

immediate and intense attachment to my favorite hunter, a bay mare named MoAlla. She was an unlikely candidate for affection, a horse with a penchant for making terrifying faces at all creatures great and small who invaded her space uninvited ... particularly during feeding time.

I'd never owned cats before I acquired a farm. Long-term country dwellers had told me that if I was going to keep my very own horses in my very own barn, I'd need my very own cat. Cats, in fact, as one cat would be lonesome and would need back-up for mouse invasions.

Obediently, I acquired a pair of kittens from the local animal shelter. They were tiny, fluffy and entirely too young and too cute to be thrust into a working barn. Thus they lived in the house for a long, long time. And when given the choice, they made it quite clear they preferred the comforts of a couch to a hay bale. Put outside day after day, they simply became porch cats.

In frustration, I obtained two more cats ... cats that had experience on their resumes as "good mousers." Simultaneously, I discovered it totally unnecessary to ever purchase a cat when you own a farm. It is, indeed, auto-matically assumed that if you have a barn you won't mind having an extra cat. I ended up with six before discovering owning acreage and outbuildings didn't necessarily make you a cat depository and learned to say "NO!"

My cats developed into more than adequate barn help until the weather turned bitter. Then, no matter how hard I tried to convince them the hayloft was very warm even on the coldest nights, they became garage cats and, more often, part-time house cats.

Then Farley appeared in our lives. He was mostly Siamese, with mostly Siamese markings and color and brilliant blue eyes. I say "mostly," because I believe that was the reason Farley was thoughtlessly dropped from a car that paused at a stop sign. Obviously, some Midnight Skulker had romanced a pure Siamese and Farley was the unwelcome result. We rescued him, standing confused and chagrined on the shoulder of the road, and brought him home on the premise that he would only be a barn cat.

As it turned out, he wouldn't have it any other way. Arriving home, I slid open the barn door and deposited Farley on the floor. He turned to look at me with those perfect azure eyes, glared at each of the four curious barn cats in turn, and hopped up on the door of MoAlla's stall. Gazing at her for a brief moment, he skittered along the boards and hopped straight onto her (thankfully) blanketed back.

I held my breath as I waited for MoAlla to snatch the intruder and fling him against the side of her stall. Her stall was where she ate, and she had a great attachment to her hay rack, her feed tub and even her water bucket. Should one of the dogs that often accompanied me to the barn unthinkingly and unwisely go into her stall while I was feeding, MoAlla would flatten her ears and dive for the curious canine. This applied to the cats as well, though they quickly learned to avoid her territory. She once even attached a feckless rooster who bopped in searching for dropped pieces of grain. He escaped with fewer tail feathers and a permanent limp.

Therefore, when Farley perched on her back my heart missed a beat or two. Rousing MoAlla's ire could have made being dropped on the road seem like the high point of his day. She stopped eating her hay mid-mouthful, swung her head around and stared at Farley, aghast at his audacity. Finding, perhaps, she simply couldn't outstare those incredible eyes, or deciding the cat was no threat to her hay consumption, or whatever her equine reasoning, she allowed him to remain on her back.

When I fed that evening, Farley was curled on MoAlla's rump, fast asleep. I fed the other cats first, scooping tasty fish parts in a large dish. While Farley deigned to open one lovely eye, he decided he wasn't meant to eat from a communal cat dish. After the others finished supper, he simply stood on MoAlla's back, stretched elegantly and hopped over to finish up the delicacies ... alone.

I dumped grain in the tubs, shook out hay and was filling water buckets when Farley decided to take up his post again. This time he walked straight across MoAlla's hay, leapt on the edge of her precious feed tub (unaware this could mean certain death), and resumed his position on her rump. As the weeks and months passed, Farley roamed freely through MoAlla's habitat, often while she was eating, fearlessly wandering through her legs and near her teeth, never once considering he could be skirting disaster.

When the weather turned warm, MoAlla shed her blankets, but she didn't shed Farley. He continued curling up and sleeping on her back with the mutual understanding that he'd keep his claws sheathed if she wouldn't roll over on him.

As the horses spent more and more time outdoors, so did Farley. He wasn't missed in the barn, having never worked an honest day in his life. Mice could, and did, actually scoot directly beneath his whiskers, only to have Farley gaze haughtily at the ceiling, clearly if silently, stating he "didn't do mice." He had hired himself out as MoAlla's companion. Period.

Farley could often be found lying parallel on the fence rails, just near where MoAlla grazed. As she moved along, cropping grass, his furry body inched across the rail, following her like an overgrown caterpillar.

The almost-Siamese enjoyed lungeing MoAlla, too. He'd sit beside me as she went 'round and 'round so he could keep a good eye on her. He heartily disapproved of my taking her off to ride or hunt, however. He'd sometimes walk right on the trailer behind me, glaring nastily when I removed him and put him in the tack room with the door firmly shut. Once, when I left for a joint meet out of state, Farley went on a weekend hunger strike, refusing even the tastiest seafood delights until MoAlla returned to her stall. While he would probably have enjoyed it, I refused to hunt with a cat attached to my pommel.

One evening when I went to feed, I noticed Farley was nowhere to be found. He'd been on his post in the morning, but by nightfall still could not be found anywhere on the farm. MoAlla fretted. She picked at her grain and wouldn't touch her hay. True love had surfaced in this grumpy old mare. She preferred her friend to her dish. We searched everywhere, calling neighbors and driving for miles in all directions. We notified the ASPCA, put an ad in the paper immediately and notices up in the post office, the general store and the pharmacy.

MoAlla ate, but sparingly. She was disinterested, she nickered and ran in her field. Things were getting desperate, and just as we had all but given up hope (six days later), Farley appeared, walking unsteadily up the long lane to the farm.

It was during a horrendous thunderstorm, and I'd gone out to the barn to make sure the doors were securely latched. And there I spotted him, soaked to his skin, much thinner than the previous week, and with a long cut down his leg. He limped to the door, somehow managing to look regal even in his bedraggled state. I scooped Farley up joyously and took him into the house to clean him up and dress his damaged leg. Then I fed him some warm milk, bedded him in a deep box filled with blankets and wondered where he'd been.

The feed truck had come the day he disappeared. Had he gotten into the back of it? Had someone picked him up on one of his brief constitutionals without MoAlla?

It was impossible to tell, and Farley wasn't talking. He also wasn't staying in his comfortable box. He stood by the door and yowled in that peculiar Siamese voice, unwilling to compromise and sleep indoors where it was warm and dry.

I finally relented, picking him up and carrying him down to the barn where he was welcomed with a rapturous whinny from his best friend. His stiff, heavily bandaged leg made it impossible for him to hop up on his familiar perch. Undaunted, Farley strolled into MoAlla's stall and curled up smack dab in the middle of her prize flake of alfalfa.

MoAlla nuzzled him softly as he put his head down wearily between his paws. Still wet, painfully thin and slightly damaged, he seemed blissfully unaware of anything except the fact that he was home where he belonged. Farley drifted off to sleep in the middle of MoAlla's dinner, and she didn't mind at all. ☾

Cooky McClung has been writing for The Chronicle of the Horse *for about 20 years and also writes for* Practical Horseman *and* Horse Scene. *She is the author of three books:* **Horsefolk Are Different, Horsefolk Are Still Different,** *and* **Plugly, The Horse That Could Do Everything**. *Cooky is features editor for*

The Kent News *in Chestertown, MD. She has raised seven children, a zillion horses, dogs and cats, and a goat or two on farms in Maryland and Pennsylvania, and has hunted for years with packs all over the country and in Ireland.*

God forbid that
I should go to any heaven
where there are no horses.

R.B. Cunningham-Graham

Irish

By Dee Dee Hunter

It all began when I was six years old and starting riding lessons at Warelands Farm. I had taken up riding the year before, along with my older sister and brother. The first barn that we went to was all right for them, but being so small, I became frightened in the indoor arena with all the horses going their own ways. Soon my mom found a place that she thought would better suit our needs.

The new farm, Warelands, was a wonderful place. The main house had been there since the late 1600s, with bits and pieces added as needed. The horses were kept in two barns, and it seemed to me that the pastures were endless. There was a big sand ring for lessons and lots of jumps set out in a field for the older kids.

My new instructor knew everything about horses and riding, or so it seemed to me. We talked a little about the riding I had done before and she told me that I was going to ride Irish. He was a white horse but people called him gray. I thought that he was the biggest thing that I had ever seen with four legs. In fact, Irish was a Thoroughbred who had spent years in the show ring. He stood something over 16 hands and, even in retirement, could jump a 3'6" course with ease. He was the horse of choice for teaching beginners, as he was blessed with a loving nature and a sense of responsibility for small riders. Older kids could also learn a lot from him, because he associated riding ability with weight, and the heavier you were, the more difficult he could become.

I remember being frightened, but my instructor told me that Irish would take care of me, and he did. I was pretty small at that time and could only reach Irish's legs and the bottom of his stomach without standing on a box or getting one of the older kids to help me.

During my first lesson, I was doing walk and some trot on the lunge line and was wobbling all over the place. My mom said that I looked like a rag doll on the horse. My instructor explained that the posting would come more easily with practice, but I felt so vulnerable way up on top of that horse. Sure enough though, it did get easier. I began to get more confident; at one moment, I stopped paying attention, lost my balance and nearly fell off. It was as if Irish knew what was happening and moved under me to keep me from falling. It was the first time that I realized that a horse and I could be a team and help each other.

The next weekend I had another lesson on Irish. During this second lesson I did not lose my balance. My riding lesson soon became the one thing that I looked forward to most each week. By the time school was out for the summer, I was off the lunge line and steering Irish around the whole ring. I was making a lot of progress on Irish because I really trusted that horse.

With school finished for the summer, I was able spend more time at the barn. I began to learn the thousand and one things that go with horse care—how to groom them, clean stalls, clean tack and do basic leg wrapping. Whenever I had a choice of which horse to work with, I always chose Irish. Of course, our relative sizes made for some interesting changes in the usual routine. I had to get help putting his saddle on and brushing his back. I could only braid halfway up his mane, even standing on the box. My hands were too small to hold his feet, so when I picked out his hooves I had to find someone else to hold each foot.

Warelands Farm had a day camp during the summer months. My mom asked me if I wanted to go to camp there when we returned from our vacation on Cape Cod. I was a little shy about the idea of going to camp, but I did ask my mom to find out which horse I would be riding. At the end of my next lesson she asked my instructor about that and was told that I would be riding Irish. That settled it. Right away I said, "yes."

During camp I met a lot of other riders. My group was made up of people who were pretty close to my age, and we all rode at about the same level. Each student rode for half an hour with an instructor; after that time, we worked in the barn—learning stable management, the points of the horse, and elementary first aid for horses. I may have been a little ahead of the group because of the time I had spent at the barn before camp started. Once, when we were getting Irish ready, one of the counselors asked if anyone knew how to pick out a hoof. I was the only one who knew but I still needed help picking up those massive feet. Irish just stood there with a faintly amused expression in his eye, watching two people doing the job of one.

I can still remember the first time I cantered, sitting up on Irish's back and watching the world whiz by. Some of the other kids were nervous, but I knew that he would do all he could to keep me on. I also remember when I was first allowed to bring him in from the pasture by myself. I felt so proud leading him up to the barn. Irish was so gentle and calm with all of us as if he understood his responsibility as our first teacher.

I continued with lessons that fall and into the winter. The following spring, I was promoted to riding another horse, but, as Irish was still my favorite, I made a point of spending all the time with him that I could. I attended summer camp again and even though I was no longer in the beginners' group, I rode Irish from time to time. As I began jumping crossrails, it seemed to me that Irish was the most wonderful jumper in the world.

Autumn arrived, school started again, and my visits to the barn came only on weekends. My sister, brother and I had our lessons on Saturday, but sometimes on Sundays we would go over to Warelands for a free ride. On one such occasion, I ran down to the barn to see Irish but noticed that he wasn't in his stall. He wasn't in the paddock either; I could not imagine where he was. Then I saw my instructor walking him around in a circle.

Irish didn't look well. His eyes were dull, with dark circles around them. My instructor told me that Irish had colic, and I remembered having learned about that at camp. We had been taught that colic was a serious disease, but it had never occurred to me what serious meant until I saw Irish that day. I wanted to help more than anything in the world, and my instructor said that I could walk him around in the ring, but that I must keep Irish walking and not let him stop, lie down or roll. We walked and walked. The vet came and gave Irish some medicine. As the vet and my instructor talked, they looked very serious, but I could not hear what they were saying. In the course of the afternoon, almost all of the regular barn kids turned up—some for lessons, some to take turns walking Irish. It seemed to go on forever, just walking him around the ring as he followed along with sad eyes, breathing heavily.

By late in the afternoon, I had to go home. I handed Irish back to my instructor and said good-bye to both of them. On the way home I asked my mom if Irish would be okay. She told me that he was really sick but that the vet was doing all that he could.

When we got home, I went straight up to my room so I could be alone. I had never thought that anything bad could happen to Irish. It was scary and painful, and I just wished that it would go away, but there was a piece of me that was not sure what was going to happen.

The following day when I came home from school, my mom told me that Irish had died. Right then I ran up to my room and cried. It was not the type of crying that you do when you get a cut; it was the type of crying that you do when someone you love has just died. I can still remember that I cried every night before I went to bed for two weeks.

Irish was buried behind the ring. I remember that someone had made a special plaque with his name and a painted picture of him on it. It was never put outside by his grave, but stayed on the windowsill up in the farmhouse so that it would not be ruined by the weather.

Now I am almost 14, and I still remember vividly the day that I walked Irish around the ring and the night that I was told he had died, as if these things happened last week. I can remember being so small that I could hug his foreleg and look straight at his elbow. And I remember the heavy breathing and the sad eyes of our last time together. Since those two weeks, I have never cried for so long or so hard.

I can also remember that special closeness that I felt with Irish. He taught me to trust a horse and what it meant to work as a team, and that is a priceless thing to have learned at such a young age. And even now, when I close my eyes, I can still feel the rhythm of his trot. ⬧

Dee Dee Hunter is in the 7th grade and has been riding since she was 6 years old. She takes part in a variety of sports. Dee Dee's father is an artist and her mother is an art historian; she has one brother and one sister. Dee Dee has three goals for when she grows up: to become the first woman President, to become a veterinarian, and to own a barn—maybe even go into the Olympics as a equestrian team member.

Farewell to My Horse

By Frances Wilbur

Now spark your hooves upon celestial stones;
Drink deep of heaven's pure air.
Now you are strong again, forever free
To race the wind and leap the clouds
On wings which you, on earth, gave to me.

Your former friends will nicker as you canter in
To welcome you to pastures always green
And they will show you where to drink from crystal streams
Take care, dear horse, I'll ride you in my dreams. ♘

Frances Wilbur has many years of experience as a rider and as co-owner/director of Cielo Azul Ranch, a riding school and children's horsemanship camp. Frances is the author of the book, **Guide for Parents of Horse Crazy Kids**.

Dolly
The Wonder Mare

By Dr. Patricia Sullivan

The first time I laid eyes on her, my thoughts were far from what they would be months later. She was huge, imposing, pushy, had no personalit, and was in the pasture with my carefully bred warmbloods. Her name was Dolly, a 16+ hand gray Percheron. She had been leased by my train-er, Kathy Daly, to produce an Arab-cross foal.

She had no equine social skills, knowing that no matter what, she was the "boss mare." I actually feared for my mares' safety. After the dust settled, and Dolly was indeed in charge, the mares went back to their routine of grazing, coming in to eat, getting groomed, then starting all over again.

Foaling season arrived, and the first foal expected in this group of mares was a Capitol Hill foal out of my Main Marebook Thoroughbred, Tiara Fox ("Tina"). I had owned Tina's dam. I had delivered Tina. I had buried Tina's dam two years later, after a tragic thunderstorm accident.

Tina was raised with love and respect. Originally bred for racing, I quickly realized that I could not feel good about the lifestyle she would have to tolerate. Changing plans, Tina became an event horse and jumper. As Tina aged, I decided I wanted a few foals from her to carry on her bloodlines. Tina was inspected at the Holsteiner approval, the only Thoroughbred entered in the Main Marebook at that site. That year, she tied for fourth in the country, for foundation mares.

Since this was Tina's third foal, the actual foaling was a nonevent. Tina foaled in the large field at 6 a.m. on April 15. No problems, no surprises. The filly was bay, elegant, and had a beautiful face. Needing a barn name, I named her "Nikki."

All was well, the filly growing and developing.

Friendly and gentle, Nikki was handled daily. After a week, they were re-introduced into the herd. The other two mares were quite interested, but Tina would not allow them to get too near. After another week, Nikki would stay with each of the other mares while Tina grazed nearby. Babysitting was now acceptable with Tina.

Britannia was the next to foal, producing a huge filly by Le Santo on May 4. Britannia had a hard time with this delivery since the filly was so large. It was necessary for Britannia, and her foal Natalie, to stay in the stall and small paddock area, until Britannia fully recovered.

Meanwhile, Tina, Nikki, and Dolly were getting along very well. Nikki would visit Dolly often. Although Dolly was assertive over Tina, she was quite gentle with Nikki.

On May 20, I got a phone call at my office. Tina had stopped breathing. I was in shock. Tina was only 15 and seemed in excellent health. This could not be. Driving out to the farm, I kept thinking that it had to be a mistake. But when I arrived, and saw the stillness of her body, I knew it was time to say my good-byes and turn my attention to her orphaned foal.

Nikki, 4 weeks old, was confused. Her mother

would not get up and she was thirsty. She went over to Dolly and laid down beside her and took a nap. Dolly watched over her carefully. Nikki did not try to nurse from Dolly, instead, she called constantly for her mom.

Since Dolly was still at least one week from foaling, but bagged up, we could not take a chance that Nikki would drain the precious colostrum that Dolly's foal would need. We separated them in adjoining stalls. Nikki hugged the wall next to Dolly, and Dolly did the same. Fortunately, Nikki had been eating grain for two weeks. We weren't quite sure what was coming next, but felt good that at least Nikki was familiar with grain.

After talking to the vet, we tried to get Britannia to adopt Nikki. We milked her, and poured the milk on Nikki. Then, holding Britannia, we introduced Nikki to the mare and foal. Britannia would have been happy to accept her, if they had been out together before now, but Britannia's difficult delivery had kept them apart from the rest of the horses. Britannia was fine with Nikki being around her, but got quite upset when Nikki got close to her foal, Natalie. Now we had a confused, hungry, thirsty, sticky and wet foal.

We put Nikki back into the stall next to Dolly and washed the sticky milk off of her. I drove over to the local feed store and bought bottles, lamb's nipples and mare milk replacer. Nikki would have nothing to do with it. Milk in a bucket brought the same reaction despite numerous tries. She did pick at her feed and drank water.

The next day, Kathy brought Oliver Twist (a.k.a. "Ollie") over to keep Nikki company. Ollie was an orphan, that Kathy had just purchased. He had come from a farm that kept nurse-mares, for lease. Ollie had already mastered drinking milk from a bucket, with gusto. We hoped he could teach Nikki quickly.

They got along well from the start. Ollie had brought his "nanny," Bandit, a miniature horse gelding, along. Nikki did not care for him at all, and Bandit had to stay in the next stall while Ollie was in the stall with Nikki. Ollie did teach Nikki to drink milk from a bucket the next day. Ollie succeeded where we had failed. It was still necessary to keep all the horses in the barn or the adjoining paddock. Dolly did not want Nikki out of sight, but they could not be together. Nikki bonded to Ollie and the two orphans were constant companions.

Nightime brought shuffling of locations, with Dolly in the adjoining paddock in case she foaled, and the two orphans in the larger stall. Four days after the tragedy, Dolly produced a lovely half-Arab filly. I was quite surprised at her correct conformation and substance. Bay, with a star, she looked like all three of the other foals in the barn. My son, Thomas, named her "Molly" as a barn name. It stuck. Dolly still kept an eye on Nikki in the next stall, as well as on her own foal. She accepted Ollie since he seemed to come as "a package" with Nikki.

Kathy and I decided we would raise the two orphans with the two mares and their foals. Hopefully, the mares would teach the youngsters equine manners, but they would have each other for company. We turned them all out together as soon as Molly was 4 days old. Britannia and her foal enjoyed the freedom, immensely. Dolly called to Nikki and Ollie and asked them to join her and Molly. Molly was a little "put-out" at the added company, at first. Within one hour, all three foals were being groomed, herded and protected by Dolly. Nikki decided to try to nurse, and nobody complained. Ollie followed suit.

We continued to give the two orphans two quarts of milk, four times a day in buckets, as well as grain and hay. The thinking was that if they were full from what we gave them, they would leave plenty of milk for Molly. It worked out just that way, too. Molly is a chubby filly who is definitely getting more than enough milk. Dolly's milk production has risen to the demand placed on her by her "kids." All three foals are gaining weight normally, running and playing.

Cars stream by the pasture and stop, sometimes for long periods. Occasionally, I walk up to the street to talk to the spectators. The first question they always ask is, "Are they triplets?" The local TV station came out and did a story on Dolly and her "kids," as well as the local newspaper. Dolly has followers and admirers across the country. I have gotten e-mail from well-wishers across the United States.

Needless to say, my opinion of Dolly has changed dramatically. Now, I think she was sent to us as a blessing. Dolly gets baths, grooming and treats from me, as well as the others in the barn. A true Percheron, she may never show her feelings, but we all know that she loves her "kids." ☽

Dr. Patricia Sullivan is a general practice dentist in Florida. She is also the owner of Oakleigh Sporthorses, which breeds Holsteiner, Dutch and Oldenburg performance prospects.

JB Andrew:
Wild Horse in a Tuxedo

By Diana Linkous

This is the story of a wild Mustang that was captured, tamed and went on to become a successful competitor in dressage, one of the most refined of all equestrian sports.

Andy grew up in Nevada, in the wild mountains and deserts. He was a big colt for a wild horse, but early in this century, farmers who were switching to tractors had turned out their draft horses, and undoubtedly some of these horses were in his family background. The Bureau of

Land Management (BLM) watches over America's wild horses; when there are too many in an area and not enough food and water for all of them, the BLM workers gather up some of them and offer them to the public for adoption.

Andy was captured in Winnemuca, Nevada, when he was around six months old. He was sent to Palomino Valley, just half an hour south of his home where he was chosen to be part of the prisoner rehabilitation program. At the time, he was not old enough to go to the program, so he spent over a year in a holding facility in Muleshoe, Texas. When he went to the prison, he was halter broke by the women and saddle broke by the men. The black colt grew to stand 16.3-hands high and weigh nearly 1,900 pounds (almost a ton!).

Ginger Scott adopted Andy when he was 2½ years old. She had already picked out a horse on her first visit but that horse had not been thought trainable. She was back a second time and did not see any that caught her eye until someone rode up on this big, black, gangly Mustang. Ginger said it was love at first sight. They tried to talk her out of adopting him, saying his head was too big and his feet were huge (he wears a size 5 shoe, which is a BIG horse shoe!), but she insisted he was the horse for her. When

Andy was adopted, Ginger named him JB Andrew—the "JB" stands for Jail Bird. She was a Western rider, and the trainer at the barn told her he was not suitable for Western and to try dressage. That is how Ginger and Kelly O'Leary met; they shared the same trainer. Kelly's horse was lame and she needed a horse to ride; Ginger had family issues to take care of and needed someone to ride Andy.

"When I first started riding Andy," Kelly later said, "he did not have much of a personality. He would stand very quietly in the aisle and did not interact much with anyone. Over the years, and I can not pinpoint at what point it changed, Andy began to watch those around him, and would seek attention with his head by putting it (sometimes forcefully) towards you. He loves me to hug his head. Remember his head is half my height! He loves to nuzzle the back of my neck and to play with my hair." Andy loves treats—carrots, apples, cookies, bran mashes, beer, soda pop, and donuts. Kelly doesn't approve of all of those treats, so somewhere along the line, Andy must have convinced somebody to cater to his tastes!

In Kelly's words: "When I first started riding Andy he was very unbalanced. He was a Training/First Level horse. He was only 3 years old when I started to ride him, so his being unbalanced was not that uncommon." Kelly began showing him in dressage and in 1990, he took first place in AHSA First Level, Region 8. By 1994, Andy had progressed through Second Level (1st place Region 8), Third Level (1st place Region 8 and Reserve Champion in Region 5), and into Prix St. Georges. In 1999, he showed successfully in Intermediaire I and Kur (Kur is a marvelous test in which the horse performs at anywhere from Second Level to the top levels, but with music and a freestyle pattern), as well as giving demonstrations.

Andy is easy to sit at both the trot and canter. He is now schooling at Grand Prix, and his piaffe and passage work have given him a little more spring in his step. His favorite movements are the flying changes—he finds them easy to do. Andy is now 15 years old, and will be competing in Intermediaire II in 2000.

Andy is an ambassador for American's Mustangs, performing his beautiful dressage movements to music and winning fans all over the country in special exhibitions as well as competitions. There is a Breyer model of him (Number 943, discontinued in 1997), and the BLM has a collectible card for Andy. Eventually, he and Kelly became such good friends that Ginger sold him to Kelly. Andy's a friendly guy and has very good manners. But hey, if you wear a tuxedo, you have to be a gentleman! ♘

A rider and horsewoman since childhood, Diana Linkous especially loves the Thoroughbred and the Mustang. She feels that something about the spirits of both are elevating to the human spirit. Diana's first horse was a Thoroughbred mare off the track, as is her current horse. Diana has owned, as part of a small partnership, a few racehorses and enjoyed "the game." She was mentored in the ways of wild horses by Barbara Eustis-Cross, co-author of **The Wild Horse: An Adopter's Manual**.

Terrific Jimmy

By Elizabeth I.V. Hunter

On January 29, 1988, a foal was born in West Point, Iowa. His sire was Terrific Et and his dam was Trouble Josie; his name was Terrific Jimmy. His certificate of registration with the American Quarter Horse Association describes him as a chestnut with a star, strip, and snip, no other markings. All this information does not begin to really tell the story.

I first saw Jimmy in early January, 1996. Dawn, who rode at our barn, had been looking for a horse for some time and she thought Jimmy had potential. Personally, I couldn't understand why she bought him. His coat was a dull brown, his mane was ratty and the muscles of his neck were flaccid, which emphasized his long and undistinguished topline. His feet were a mess, and he had the ground manners of Attila the Hun. For all of that, however, he did have a cute face and a good eye.

As the winter wore on and spring arrived, Jimmy began to change. His coat improved with a good diet and much brushing. Some attention from the farrier, as well as time, became apparent in a better-looking hoof. He was still no bargain in the manners departmen,t but he was manageable. Since Dawn rode him almost daily, he began to get into shape. Jimmy seemed to have strong preferences about when and where he was ridden. His favorite time was 9 in the morning and he preferred not to be ridden near the bushes at the end of the ring. He was less than enthusiastic about trail rides, and was clearly appalled by mailboxes with balloons tied to them, or by babies in strollers, or by umbrellas.

By early summer, Jimmy had his owner well trained so that she did what he wanted and accepted his determination of when he had had enough. Dawn had done a lot of riding in a Western saddle and thought that some of his idiosyncratic behavior could be explained by early training out west, but when she rode him in our barn's fun show and he flat out refused to go anywhere near the barrels in the barrel racing class, we all figured that that was not an area where he had had any experience.

I had been half-leasing another horse at the barn until June, but since that horse was not available over the summer, I had to content myself with a decreasing number of rides, even as the weather was getting more and more inviting. By mid-July, I was feeling rather sorry for myself; when I heard Dawn say that she was looking for someone to ride Jimmy while she was on vacation, I decided that it might be worth investigating the possibility. We agreed on a half-lease for the month of August and, armed with copious instructions, I started to get to know the horse.

Ours was not always a smooth relationship, but we did get along in our fashion. After the first week, Jimmy realized that he could be ridden in the afternoon, past the bushes at the end of the ring, and near people with umbrellas. He also discovered that he could put his head down, could manage a regular two-beat trot, and could bend to the left. I discovered that I could not stay on when he did a sliding stop followed by a 180-degree turn. I actually wondered where he had learned that trick and why he had been taught it in the first place, but my primary interest was in getting him not to do it. Success was illusory for some time, but that did not really matter because by the end of the third week of August, I was hooked. I came to love Jimmy for what he could be, but more importantly, for what he was.

When Dawn came back from vacation, saddened because she had to sell Jimmy due to serious changes in her circumstances, I was able to say with enthusiasm that I would buy him. The deal was done and he changed hands on Labor Day in 1996.

Five days after I bought him, Jimmy pulled his right hind suspensory ligament. I thought that was a fairly unusual injury and so did the vet. But in retrospect, it was a characteristic thing for my horse to do. He recuperated nicely from that injury and then, on his first day off stall rest, he managed to become caste in the paddock that had been specially built so that he could be turned out without fear of injury. There was no serious damage done, but I was learning to be careful.

Since Jimmy was apt to get excited if he was on the

crossties facing out the barn door, I always used the ties that faced inward, toward the stalls and the grain room. It was on those crossties, facing in what we all thought was the "safe" direction, that he managed to put his right front foot up and over the crosstie and then, in a panic, to flip over backward. It was a terrifying experience for both of us. I remember how time seemed to slow to a crawl as I watched my horse rear up and pull back with all his might. He seemed to balance for a moment and then fell backward with a floor-shaking thud. He lay still for what must have only been a few seconds, but that seemed an eternity, and then got to his feet as if that were the most natural thing in the world to do. Jimmy stood looking at me, head down, eyes calm. Slowly I walked over and took hold of his halter, patted his neck and walked him forward a few steps. Apart from a nasty cut on his forehead, right in the center of the star, he seemed fine. Fortunately the vet was close by and sewed the cut within an hour of the injury. I was warned that the hair might not grow back, but it did in the end, so one needs to look very closely to see the scar. Conveniently, when the vet came back to take out the stitches, he was able to remove the cyst that my trainer had discovered inside his right nostril. He took his second surgery very well; I suspect that he liked the recuperative attention. But at that point I was wondering what else could go wrong with my horse.

That first six months set a record for vet calls which, fortunately, we have not repeated. I have learned that my horse will, in the manner of a small child, get involved in any trouble that presents itself. As a result of this insight, I am very, very careful to be sure that there are no attractive hazards around Jimmy and that every piece of equipment that he uses is in the best possible shape. Some people and some horses can get away with cutting corners because they have incredible luck. Jimmy and I have to be careful because we are incredibly accident-prone.

With spring came soundness, and Jimmy and I began working together seriously. It was not always an easy process. After several really frustrating weeks, I called information to get the number of Jimmy's breeder to see if he could give me any insight into my horse and his history. We had a long conversation, which ended with my getting the telephone number of the person who Jimmy had been sent to for his early training. And that call led to others, so that the horse's history began to become clear.

As it turned out, Jimmy had led the pampered life of

a conformation competitor for the first four years of his life. At that point he began training as a barrel racer, something that he didn't really seem to enjoy much and at which he did not excel. I think it was at this period that he mastered the sliding stop/quick turn routine which is so effective when he has had enough of just about anything. While he was in training, his owner died and the owner's widow, faced with a seemingly overwhelming number of horses, sold most of them to a dealer from the East. Jimmy stayed on the dealer's lot for about a year and a half, living out with a large group of other horses and not receiving any special attention. In the end, a woman who thought that he had possibilities bought him. As it turned out, however, his new owner was also newly pregnant, and therefore had little time to put into his training. It was that woman who had sold him to Dawn who brought him to our barn. I knew and was a part of his history from that point on. I found all this information useful, but to this day I wonder when those sliding stops and 180-degree turns came into his repertoire.

For his part, Jimmy has been working hard to train me to stay exactly over his center of gravity. He is happiest and best able to concentrate on the task at hand when I, his rider, am in balance and able to ride him between the aids. Teaching me to do that has taken a great deal of patience, since my previous riding experience was all forward seat and no dressage. We are working on it and "making good progress," as the teachers of small children are apt to write on report cards.

Three years and four months into our partnership, I think both Jimmy and I can be proud of our success thus far. He has gone from being the horse that children are warned to stay away from to being the barn pet. Under saddle he is, for the most part, a willing participant who enjoys his work, especially if there is jumping involved. He is not a great trail horse because of the "lions" in the woods and the horse-eating trolls that hide behind blowing leaves. But he is getting better at going out, so long as there are no balloons or roller bladers in stealth mode. For my part, I am relearning how to ride and am in the process getting better at it. We won a ribbon at a local schooling event and might even try a jumper show this spring. But there are still days when a cold wind sends the clouds scudding along the sky, and the trolls and lions may be about. So on those days, we stay in the ring and share carrots afterward. ☕

Elizabeth Hunter is a middle-aged amateur who has been riding since she was 10, with a long timeout to raise three children. A graduated Pony Club "B," she is presently working very hard to bring her riding level up to the expectations of her horse.

There is no secret quite so close as that between a rider and his horse.

Robert Smith Surtees

Magic Moments

By Marianne Alexander

I founded Personal Ponies Ltd., Inc. to benefit disabled and/or terminally ill children by offering a tiny pony for life use. There is no charge. It is a well-known saying that "the outside of a horse is good for the inside of a man." As founder of the Personal Ponies program, I had noted for quite some time a very real lack of attention to the needs of young special-needs children and the absence of suitably small equines bred just for them. Surely "the outside of a pony would be good for the inside of a small child who is differently able."

We have many stories to tell about ponies and kids and the seemingly wonderful miracles that happen when a little special child and a little special pony become friends.

Brittoni

Recently, a 28-inch pony named Clementine was sent to Brittoni, a five-year-old girl who is blind and deaf. Most of Brittoni's brain is deteriorated from the abuse she suffered when she was only two weeks old. Brittoni, who cannot say, "mama," spends her days wearing her hard hat, sitting by the pony paddock, singing, "Oh My Darlin' Clementine," at the top of her lungs.

Peter

Muffy was barely a week old. She didn't quite measure 13 inches tall and weighed a mere 16 pounds, tiny even by Miniature Shetland standards. Friends asked if they could visit Greystone Farm with a couple from South America who had a little boy who was very ill. We weren't told what the illness was, only that they wished their young son to see the small ponies.

The father carried the baby, who was perhaps a year old, into Muffy's stall where she lay near her mother,

Cupcake. We placed the little boy, only a baby himself, on the straw near Muffy, and we were shocked when she lay her own little head on the baby's chest. Cupcake stood nearby and watched.

For perhaps five minutes, there was total silence. Nothing moved. There was not a single sound. Then the father gathered up his son and carried him to the car. As we watched the father and his son settle into the car, I looked with the mother at the little boy's face. There were tears running down his pale cheeks. The mother turned to me and said quietly, "I have never before seen Peter cry."

I do not know what passed between this tiny pony and this small boy, but surely we witnessed something very special. We were told later that Peter died that week.

Mary

Mary got her pony, Merry Meadow, on Christmas Eve. She and her mother had plotted and planned for six weeks for this special arrival. They bought purple buckets and a purple pony wardrobe and put up fences and a stall. But best of all, not only was Mary getting her very own pony, but soon there would be two ponies to care for because her pony was pregnant!

And just as planned, a horse trailer arrived on Christmas Eve and out came Merry Meadow jingling with the sound of bells on her halter and festooned with Christmas ribbons. Mary could not see her pony as she stepped down from the trailer because she is blind—but she could hear her bells and the patter of her tiny, pony feet.

For many hours that night, Mary hugged and brushed her new pony and marveled at the hay-sweet warmth of her pony breath and the fuzzy, round belly that sheltered a new life. It was early morning before Mary turned out the barn lights and headed toward the house.

Mary and her mother had planned to breed ponies for other blind children. Their dream was cut short, however, when Mary died unexpectedly that Christmas Day. Mary's mother wrote to us about the tragic ending to this story, but she also told us how comforting it was for her that Mary experienced the magic of her own special pony—if only for a few short hours.

Mary's mother has decided to keep Merry Meadow and to continue to breed ponies for other blind children in Mary's memory.

Mitchell

Mitchell had never talked. Not ever. And he was seven years old. His mother also told us that he seldom cried. On occasion, though, he smiled and laughed. Maybe a visit to a pony farm would be something for Mitchell to smile about.

Jenny brought Muffy, our 23-inch black mare down the drive toward Mitchell who was standing by the big rock. Almost at once, Mitchell threw his arms in the air and wound them around Muffy's short, furry neck. Then, as he buried his face in her mane, we all heard him cry, "Oh, pony!" We were all stunned, but Mitchell's mother nearly fainted! She turned to me immediately and asked if she could buy Muffy, but I had to explain to her that Muffy is a permanent part of Greystone Farm and is not for sale. We did, however, make sure this story had a happy ending because a kind and gentle gelding named Daisy Dan soon became Mitchell's pony companion.

We receive many letters about Mitchell and Daisy Dan, who now takes the little boy out for pony rides. Daisy Dan pulls a cart, too, and sometimes visits Mitchell's class at school. But the letter we like best tells how Daisy Dan comes into the kitchen for cornflakes and apples in his very own bowl.

And Mitchell? Oh, he hasn't stopped talking!

Marianne Alexander is the founder and Executive Director of Personal Ponies Ltd., Inc., a non-profit organization that donates miniature Shetland ponies to children with disabilities. Now in its four-teenth year, Personal Ponies has enriched the lives of numerous children and their families. To find out more about Personal Ponies, contact Marianne at (607) 844-9300.

American Pie

By Elisabeth Austin

Sometimes horses go through their lives without ever finding that one special person who will bring out the best in them. For a little buckskin named American Pie, I am that person. This story isn't just about our success in the show ring; rather, it is the tale of an underdog who, with correct training and lots of love, became a champion in more ways than one.

Pie was born as a result of a scientific field test. The now famous Equitainer, used for artificial insemination, was field tested in Vermont. Semen from the Hamilton Farm stallions was shipped in the prototype Equitainer to any mare owner who took part in the program. Draft mares, Morgan mares, Thoroughbred mares—a wide variety of breeds were used. Unless they paid a breeding fee, mare owners did not know to which stallions their mares had been bred. It wasn't very hard to figure out, though, as you could pretty much guess who sired who, given the strong characteristics of the stallions.

Pie's mother was an Arabian/Quarter Horse-cross named Savannah Blue. Savannah's owner bought her specifically to be used in this breeding program. Apparently, Savannah gained a reputation as a bad-tempered horse due to the fact that she was so protective of Pie when he was born. Today, she is a very reliable and quiet trail horse for her owner.

Pie's father was the Trakehner stallion Karneval. Known for his good movement and attractive offspring, Karneval was a successful FEI dressage horse before being retired to teach many people to ride upper-level movements.

Pie's breeder, Edith Taylor, actually named him Kloyo when he was a foal. She worked for a Dutchman in

New York while Pie was a foal and he called him something that sounded like Kloyo. It might have been "kleurig," which is the Dutch word for "colorful." As luck would have it, Pie turned out to be buckskin, even though his parents were gray and chestnut.

Pie first came into our lives when he was three years old. Amanda Warrington, who was living in Vermont at that time, wanted a young horse to bring along to compete in high level eventing. While Amanda was in Vermont she was a student of my mom's; she and my mom went to look at Pie together.

As soon as Amanda saw the flashy buckskin gelding, she knew she had to have him, and bought him right there on the spot. Pie came to live at the farm the next week. When Amanda and my mom free-jumped him for the first time, they couldn't believe how clever and talented he was. It appeared that he had a wonderful future ahead of him.

Pie was very talented as a youngster. He was eager to learn and wanted to be kept busy. His training progressed quickly and, by the following summer when Amanda returned to her home in Massachusetts, Pie was ready to begin competing. Amanda started him out in some low-level events and did very well. She moved him up to Training Level that fall.

By the next spring, Amanda felt that Pie was ready to go Preliminary. At this level, the horses have to jump 3'9" fences and do a First Level dressage test. By all indications, Pie should have had no trouble with this level. But somewhere along the way, Pie lost his confidence. He could and did jump all the fences, at least for awhile. After he did more shows though, Pie decided that the dressage was something he was no good at, and he became increasingly tense and nervous every time he had to enter the arena.

My mom saw Pie a few times during this period at competitions during which Amanda had asked for training. Pie would go down the centerline in the dressage arena and basically canter in place or sideways. His body was never in the same place twice and he looked completely miserable. Amanda was becoming increasingly frustrated and upset with him. She could deal with him being impossible to ride on the flat, but she decided he wasn't going to be the event horse she had hoped for after he began stopping over fences as well.

Pie was put on the market for sale, but instead of selling him right away, Amanda ended up leasing him to one of her working students. Several years passed. Amanda went on to other horses and a very successful career as an international event rider.

Meanwhile, my pony Warlock and I were a perfect team. I was ten and he was 24; ours was a partnership that was seven years in the making. Warlock had done practically everything during his lifetime. He had been a Western pony, a hunter, an eventer, a school horse and now, with me, a dressage pony. Warlock took everything that came his way with equanimity. Together, we had won many ribbons in dressage competitions. Although Warlock was sound and healthy, he became very old and, as it is the way of the world, one night he lay down in his stall, and his heart stopped beating.

I was devastated. Warlock had been my dearest friend. He was kind and gentle, ever patient and understanding—what every child's first pony should be. My mom looked everywhere for another horse for me, and just as things began to look grim, she called Amanda, inquiring about a nice mare named Crocus. Amanda had evented the mare quite successfully, and she would have been a perfect horse for me, but it wasn't meant to be, as Amanda's mother was riding her. Out of curiosity, my mom asked what Pie was doing. Amanda's immediate reaction was "What on earth would you want him for?" And the rest, as they say, is history.

I clicked with Pie immediately and from that day forth it has been the kind of story you read about in magazines—the unrideable horse at the end of the line who, when befriended by someone who tells him he"s a champion, truly does become one.

In the beginning, it wasn't easy. Pie liked to do things his way, and if you asked him to do otherwise, he became tense and disobedient. He thoroughly enjoyed doing the opposite of what he was asked as far as dressage was concerned, and liked nothing more than to run like a bat out of hell when jumping.

From the start, my mom believed she had made a mistake in allowing me to ride Pie. He wanted nothing to do with dressage, and, try as I might, he was impossible for me to ride. After a few months, however, Pie was rideable enough to show. We entered him in First Level and hoped for the best. Yet as soon as we got onto the show grounds, I knew this was going to be quite a ride. Pie was nervous, whinnying frantically, and could not concentrate on anything except where the other horses were. I tried hard to keep him with me through our tests, but by that time it was a lost cause—Pie had reverted to his old, unreliable self. Needless to say, that was our first, and last, show of the year.

Through the winter we progressed quite a bit to the point where Pie wasn't always trying to avoid a steady connection, and was beginning to bring his hind legs it least somewhere in the vicinity of the rest of his body, as opposed to way out behind it. I learned that if I tapped him with the whip lightly and clucked with my voice, Pie would do a very pretty, slow, floaty trot that I thought was passage. Very excited, I showed my mom, but her reaction wasn't what I had hoped it would be. She said that it looked like Pie had the talent to learn passage, but it would be a long time before he would be ready to do it. To be honest, I don't think she planned on having him long enough to find out.

The next spring we did a small schooling show in preparation for some of the bigger shows we planned to do that year, and although it went better than our first show, Pie was still ill-behaved and anxious to see what the other horses were doing. He still neighed almost all the time, especially when other horses walked by—which, at a horse show, is a frequent event. We did a few more shows that year, but there was still a huge difference from the work we would do at home, which was relatively tension-free, to what would happen at shows, which was not a pretty sight.

Again, we worked hard throughout the winter, and I set a goal for myself of obtaining my bronze medal (two scores of 60% or above at First, Second and Third Levels) on Pie. I didn't care how long it took; it was going to happen. I was sure of it. It seemed as if the winter of 1995-1996 was different than the previous winter. Something had clicked for Pie and me. Maybe it was the fact that in February of 1996, we got the call that I had been dreading for two years.

I remember the day quite clearly. It was one of the warmer February days, at least by Vermont standards. I was on my way into my bedroom when my mom yelled to me from down stairs. She asked me to sit down, and I immediately could tell it was something important. "I got a call from Pie's owners today," she said, "They want him back." I almost burst into tears right there, but she quickly followed with telling me that Amanda's mom, Deirdre, had offered to sell Pie to us for less than his asking price, and we could pay it in two parts. She then continued by telling me that she had told Deirdre she'd think about it.

As one might imagine, I was an absolute "angel" for

the next week—cleaning, doing chores and other random tasks, all in hopes that my mom would allow me to keep this horse who meant so much to me. After a few days (which seemed to pass like weeks), she agreed to purchase Pie. I still tell her it's the best decision she ever made, although it has taken me quite some time to prove it. And now that Pie was officially mine, we had all the more reason to work hard and maybe, just maybe, start ourselves on our way for that bronze medal.

At the start of the 1996 show season, we once again did a schooling show. Unlike like last time, however, doing a schooling show in the beginning of the season was quite beneficial as Pie got all of his bad behavior over and done with at our very first show. The next show was our first real entry into "big-time" dressage—Dressage at Saratoga, CDI. This show was Pie's breakthrough performance, as he was nearly as nice at a show as he was at home. Before the weekend was through we had two of our scores for the bronze medal, and a ribbon from every class.

Saratoga was only a hint of what was to come. The rest of 1996 brought even more ribbons, good scores, and yet another score for the bronze medal. In 1997 we moved our farm, which was a big change for Pie. Although the new farm is only a few miles from the old, it was like night and day. The new farm offered huge open fields sprinkled with deer and wild turkey and was, best of all, quiet.

Our daily regimen consisted of a bareback gallop in the morning, work in the afternoon, another bareback gallop in the evening, and a cool bath just before bed. I don't think Pie had been that fit since his eventing days. Not only was there a change in farms, but a change in Pie, too. He was becoming happier and happier about his work, and was no longer worried or unwilling to do dressage.

The moving of the farm brought a lack of funding for our '97 show season, thus we only did one show. That show was a memorable one, however—the Region 8 Junior/Young Rider Team Championships. This was the first show that we ever did Third Level and, to my surprise, we were the champion of our division.

The following year we competed at Second and Third Levels in hopes of finally getting those last few scores for our bronze medal. While that was our only real goal of 1998, we did manage to win the Reserve Championship at Dressage at Saratoga in the Third Level Junior/Young Rider Category, as well as the New England Dressage Association Year End Award for Third Level, Junior/Young Rider. And if that wasn't enough, we nearly met our goal of the bronze medal.

It is not necessary to earn all of these scores required for the bronze medal on the same horse, but it was always my goal to get the scores on Pie alone. I was offered all sorts of horses—from nice young Dutch Warmbloods to Grand Prix school masters—to show, but I knew that in the long run, it would be much more advantageous for me if I were to train my own.

The 1999 show season was by far our best year yet. It was our first year at Fourth Level, as well as continuing with Third Level. The goal for 1999 was not only to get our bronze medal, but also to try for a spot at the 1999 Cosequin Junior Championships being held in Devon, Pennsylvania. I knew it would be difficult, but what did I have to lose, right?

Once again, we did a schooling show as a starter, followed by Dressage at Saratoga, where we were second to none, having a clean sweep of all our Third and Fourth Level classes. We also won the Third Level Junior/Young Rider Championship, $300, and lots of other goodies, giving us a total of over $500 in cash and prizes!

Probably the sweetest part of 1999 Dressage at

Saratoga wasn't the prizes or the ribbons, but the score we got on our first ever FEI Junior Individual Test, a 63%. Since the test is equal to Fourth Level, that 63% gave us the first score in the hunt for our silver medal, although it still didn't fulfill the needed last score for the bronze. Pie's ever-growing fan club came to the show to watch it all unfold—some of his online fans came specifically to watch him perform.

The rest of the show season was just as perfect as the first show, as we earned even more blue ribbons, more 60%+ scores, and the last score for our bronze medal. As of now, we're half way to our silver medal. Our average score for the show season was a 61.9%.

Although we didn't qualify for the Junior Championships at Devon, we did earn that bronze medal, which is the dearest to me of all the prizes I've won with Pie. Mainly because it doesn't represent one show or one Championship, but all of our work, from square one and up. When I look at that little bronze medal, I see much more than simply the rider and horse engraved in it. I see all of my memories with Pie, condensed—the sweat, the tears, the joy, the defeat and the victory.

The year 2000 brings many things for Pie and me.

This past April we were invited to do a clinic with one of the best trainers in the world, Conrad Schumacher of Germany. And even though we were in the company of horses who are Olympic hopefuls, and amazing riders, I didn't feel a bit out of place, because I knew I had earned my right to be there. Certainly Pie wasn't the fanciest, most talented or most impressive horse at the clinic, but he deserved to be there. In the company of rising dressage stars was my own champion. While he isn't known nationwide for his success as a dressage horse, Pie has a worldwide fan club of people six to 60 years old.

So what does the future hold? Who knows? Pie did indeed learn to passage. He now also does piaffe, tempi changes, canter pirouettes and can bow on command like there's no tomorrow.

As Pie's 16th birthday approaches, I find it a good time reflect on the nearly six years that we've been a team. Looking not only at the wins, losses and everything in between, but at the quieter moments, too. The bareback gallops at dusk, chasing deer through the meadows, not a care in the world. Or the lazy summer afternoons spent lounging in the hammock reading, Pie grazing by my side. In these moments, Pie is no longer a dressage horse, nor am

I a dressage rider. Rather, we're two good friends enjoying all that life has to offer. ♘

Elisabeth Austin was born in 1984 in Burlington, Vermont. She is currently a sophomore in high school, and hopes to go into the horse business after college. A dressage competitor since the age of seven, Elisabeth has earned her bronze medal on American Pie and is half way to her silver medal. Elisabeth and Pie will compete at Prix St. Georges in the summer of 2000, and will try for the North American Young Rider Championships in 2001.

The history of mankind
is carried on the back of the horse.

Author Unknown

Ruffian

By Diana Linkous

She was never defeated, and never headed. She set or equaled a new stakes record in every one of the eight stakes races she won. She raced at distances from 5½ furlongs to 1½ miles with an average winning margin of 8 1/3 lengths. She was queen of the track, and everyone knew it.

Ruffian was bred by Mr. and Mrs. Stuart Janney for their Locust Hill Farm, and was born in 1972 at Claiborne Farms in Kentucky. She frolicked as a filly and weanling there, and was shipped to Belmont Park in New York for schooling under the care of trainer Frank Whiteley, Jr.

Ruffian was a tall, very dark bay filly, deep-bodied but long-legged and with a long body and neck. There was no mistaking her for anything but a racehorse. She broke the track record in her first race, winning by 13 lengths. She won every race she was entered in her two-year-old season, but fractured a bone late in the year and was retired to recuperate for awhile. She was crowned two-year-old filly of the year.

The following year, 1975, people were excited to see if she would come back as good as she'd been as a two-year-old. Her running style had always been to burst like a demon from the gate and never look back, taking the lead immediately and sprinting to the end of the race. Dark lightening she was. But as a 3-year-old, the races would be longer than the six furlongs she was used to—as long as a mile and a quarter, even a mile and a half. It takes a super horse to sprint that distance. Was Ruffian a super horse?

Ruffian's first race as a 3-year-old was on April 14 in the six furlong Calthea Purse at Aqueduct, which she won by 4½ lengths. From then on, she raced at longer and longer distances, and her winning margins became increasingly longer as well. She won the seven furlong Comely Stakes by 7¾ lengths, then ten days later the 1 mile Acorn

Stakes by 8¼ lengths. Then she ran at 1 1/8 mile in the Mother Goose Stakes and came home first by 14 lengths.

In winning the Acorn and Mother Goose Stakes, Ruffian had captured the first two legs of the Filly Triple Crown. The 1½ mile Coaching Club American Oaks is the third leg, and she was ready for it. Ruffian went straight to the front, as she always did, and ignored the several persistent pursuers who flew at her. She did not even appear to be seriously pushed during these attempts to catch up to and pass her. Only one filly, Equal Change, could stay near in the closing stages, but Ruffian was clearly better, and won by 2¾ lengths.

She'd done it all. She held the Filly Triple Crown, had been Filly 2-Year-Old of the Year, and would no doubt win that title as a 3-year-old even if she never raced again. So, it was decided to put her to one more test: there would be a match race between Foolish Pleasure, that year's Kentucky Derby winner, and Ruffian. Ruffian had never raced against colts before, but she certainly seemed up to it.

Foolish Pleasure's trainer gave him a few extra sessions in breaking from the gate fast, since Ruffian seemed to win all her races by leading from the start. On July 7, 1975, more than 31,000 people watched Foolish Pleasure leap from the gate with his head in front, the first time a horse had headed Ruffian. Ruffian quickly sprinted up from the inside and stuck her head in front. Ruffian seemed to have trouble, bouncing off Foolish Pleasure for several lengths, but she increased her margin to about a half length in front as the pair approached the clubhouse turn. The crowd was cheering loudly as the race appeared to be turning into the great race they'd hoped for, two magnificent racehorses head and head the whole way.

But as the two horses approached the mile marker, there was a sound that both jockeys described later as being "like the breaking of a board," and the great match race was over. Ruffian had broken a leg. Jacinto Vasquez, Ruffian's jockey, had a terrible time pulling her up; she was fighting to continue the race despite her shattered leg.

Heroic efforts were made to save Ruffian. A pneumatic cast was applied before she was loaded onto the ambulance and a new one was applied in the barn area. A team of four veterinarians and an orthopedic surgeon worked for 12 hours to save her leg. During the operation, Ruffian stopped breathing two times and had to be revived. Finally, the surgery was done.

However, the worst was yet to come. The anesthesia wore off and the filly awoke, disoriented and confused, as is often the case with horses and anesthesia. She thrashed about wildly despite the attempts of several attendants to hold her down. In her struggles, she fractured the new cast and the opposite leg, and caused even greater damage to the original break. Knowing that she could not live through further surgery, the veterinarians had to put her to sleep to end her suffering.

Ruffian is buried near the flagpole at Belmont Park, with her nose pointed toward the finish line. The flags at Belmont flew at half-mast that day, July 7, 1975. ☙

A Matter of Trust

By Jacqueline Wall

I bought Opie (HL Open Throttle) in April of 1998. I had been looking for an Arabian to train for jumping, and he certainly fit the bill. When he first arrived, he was social enough, but he didn't quite realize that we were his new family.

Opie soon realized that I came to see him almost every day, and in no time, he began meeting me at the fence. We didn't just train for shows, but went on trail rides "just because," and some days, we just walked around as he grazed on the end of a leadrope. We became buddies and played all sorts of games. He's always greeted me, although some days we had to play tag before he would be caught.

Opie learned that I would never ask him to do something beyond his capabilities. We've built a relationship of deep trust. His trust was apparent in the way he didn't hesitate if I asked him to jump a strange fence, or the way he'd dive right into the water we had to cross. Often we'd go hill climbing, and he took me down some I didn't think we could handle. In his own way, Opie always assured me that he could handle it if I would just let him try. We learned how to listen to each other and decide how we should handle things. His willingness told me how much he loved any given challenge, especially when it came to hill climbing. That's how we got ourselves into some trouble.

In the spring of 1999, I was working at a ranch on Ft. Carson, Colorado. My primary job was to train would-be trail horses and guide trail rides. My husband volunteered on the weekends, and we often took a trail ride out together. About halfway through one such ride, everyone decided to take a break—everyone except Opie and me. I took Opie to play in the ravines while the others rested. I wasn't at all nervous as the entire area had been deemed safe for horses.

As we came up to the end of a ravine, I gave Opie his head and let him take us up the hill. Something wasn't right. His boots were caught—on the brush, maybe? Before I could do anything to stop him, he set his feet down, then lunged again. He pulled so hard, and his feet were caught so firmly, that he ultimately flipped over. As I attempted to leap up and help my horse walk off the fall, I quickly became stuck. Not wanting to get stepped on, I had him place his head on my shoulder and lie still. As I looked over his shoulder, I saw rusty barbed wire all tangled around his legs. Apparently, that's what held me, too.

Frantically, I called to my husband. Opie calmly rested his head on my shoulder while all four feet were untangled, then the saddle uncinched. He still lay on the ground while two more people helped me up. Opie didn't attempt to get up until I gave him the "okay." At that point, he stood right up and walked out.

When I examined him, I noticed a few shallow scratches on his rump, but nothing serious. However, his neoprene splint boots were shredded. I honestly believe that if he hadn't been wearing his splint boots, his legs would have been destroyed.

Some horses give their all for their owners: Opie is

certainly one of those horses. He was so willing to try with all his might to get us up that hill. His complete trust in me allowed him to stay calm while he was laying downhill, entangled and trapped in the wire. His trust is what saved his legs, if not his life. ♘

Jacqueline Wall has been riding since the age of five, and currently owns a horse and a pony. She works out of her Tennessee home, making Arabian show costumes. Jacqueline rides for pleasure and loves to show.

Mikey

By *Hilary Nolan Penlington*

I dreaded being the last to pick which school horses to use at the stable that employed me. It always seemed
that the ratio of students to horses was beyond reason-
able—for the horses, that is.

I have grown with horses for over 20 years now. In
my family, I am considered the first generation of "horse
crazed." I would ride anything that would stand still long
enough for me to mount, and valiantly try to stay aboard
anything that didn't.

Growing up, I met all types of equines: hot, cold, stubborn, weak, aggressive, passive, trained, untrained. The list goes on. After graduating from college with a bachelor's degree in Equine Science, I thought I knew it all. Little did I know I would come across a small chestnut gelding named Mikey.

After graduation I was hired on the spot at a small farm in Massachusetts. During my interview, I was introduced to all of the horses and residents of the farm. I saw several horses in good flesh, but one—Mikey—stood out like a sore thumb. Hips showing, countable ribs, pencil neck, an undulating back—a 14.2 hand bag of bones. I was told that Mikey had been rescued one step short of slaughter, and that the farm owner was trying to incorporate him into her riding program.

In the beginning, my instructions were to place multiple saddle pads on Mikey's back to fill in the sway and to use a razor-edge snaffle, as he had "a stopping problem." Oh, and don't be within any vicinity of his teeth while doing up his girth! His trot was enough to displace your lunch, but his canter was smooth as silk.

No one wanted to ride Mikey because of his trot, but moreso because of the habits he had learned out of self-preservation. He was never malicious, but knew all of the scare tactics developed from poor human skills. If you had heavy hands, he put his head to his chest and locked his jaw. If you kicked him, he took off. If you leaned too far on his neck in jumping position, he would forever speed up. This taught many children and adults that leaning was a sure way of getting run away with and ending your lesson with a concussion and a trip to the tack shop for a new helmet.

When approaching jumps, Mikey's motto was, "why bother going over when you can go around?" This was unacceptable behavior to the farm's owner, and as Mikey's popularity waned so did his care. His shoes were pulled and his grain ration dropped. The weight he had so slowly gained began to drop within a fortnight.

After two years of servitude, I came into an opportunity to purchase this business. The school horse package consisted of Mikey, presumed 18 years old, and two other equines: one very athletic, and the other nominated "pasture potato" as he was more or less a lawn ornament.

After giving him some time off, I decided to learn from Mikey. I spent time listening to what his needs were in the field and in the barn. He was much happier residing outside in the field, so there he stayed. I removed the razor snaffle bit and put him into a hackamore, which stopped him with ease. One thick western saddle blanket under his saddle seemed to suit him better than the piles that consistently bunched up on his back. What I learned about Mikey was that he was sad, starving and sore.

I had our veterinarian and farrier give me the run down on what would be best for Mikey. It was then that I discovered that my 18-year-old with "good feet" was actually in his early 30s and in the beginning stages of navicular disease.

Over the next two years we formed a trust and a friendship of give and take. I treated him with love and respect and he applied them to my students. Mikey gained over 350 pounds in the years of my charge, learned to jump for the fun of it, and carried six-year-olds to the ribbons in walk-trot classes at local shows. He reveled in the thrills of local three-phase competitions with the older students. He never allowed you to be a passenger, but was insistent in working as a partnership. I say "allowed" because, despite his trot, his wisdom to others was a gift to all who rode him.

Mikey was in my life for five short years, yet his knowledge and wisdom carries into my everyday workings with horses. In the early winter of 1998, Mikey passed over the Rainbow Bridge due to a life-ceasing colic and complications of old age. He arrived in my life with no courage, pride or dignity. He left teaching just that to all he touched, and instilled immeasurable knowledge and memories upon my soul. ☺

Hilary Nolan Penlington owns and operates Serendipity Stables in Norfolk, Massachusetts, where she trains horses and riders in dressage and combined training. A graduate of Johnson & Wales University in Rhode Island, she holds a bachelor's degree in Equine Sciences and associate's degrees in both Entrepreneurship and Equine Business Management. Hilary is also a local animal control officer and animal health inspector. She and her husband, Stephen, are the proud parents of two-year-old Patrick. Hilary credits trainers Mona Raymond and Lu Denizard with much of her success.

He doth nothing but talk of his
horses.

William Shakespeare,
The Merchant of Venice

Phoenix

By L.R. Davidson

Author's Note: This story is dedicated to the memory of Heather St. Clair Davis, who recently passed on. She always believed in me as a writer, rider, artist and performer. She was one of the bravest, kindest and most wonderful women I have ever met.

If you happen to be a horseperson, you know what it's like when you "click" with a certain horse. I think it's one of the most wonderful experiences you could have— that feeling of being so rhythmically correct with your horse that you can almost read his/her mind. It's as if you know what each other's thoughts are. You feel as one, safe, like nothing matters except you and your horse. Everything around you dissolves, as if a mirage. That's the way I felt when I first rode my pony jumper, Ruthless (better known at home as Phoenix.)

It was a bitterly cold Canadian day when I first met Phoenix. My mom and I had gone to Canada to look for pony prospects. We have a business together where we find green pony hunter/jumper prospects and I train them (along with help from my trainer, Joe Forrest), and, eventually, sell them. We do a main search about three times a year. It's amazing!

I ride about 30 to 40 ponies in one weekend, not even counting the horses I try out for other people. I love it! My mom and I always have fun. Ponies and riding are something special we share. (My dad's not into horses at all. To him they are big, stupid and dangerous!)

On that particular day, we had already tried about 10 ponies, and were in the car heading to look at another one. Mom asked me to read what she had written down about the next pony.

"13.0 hand mare," I read. "Two hind socks, big blaze. Cute jump. Would make an excellent short stirrup or pony for a beginner. Changes there when asked nicely. Name: Phoenix."

"Sounds interesting," mom replied.

We pulled into the driveway of the barn. I walked to the door leading into the indoor, and opened it. There I set eyes on the most beautiful pony I had ever seen in my life—a really refined bay with two hind white socks and a stripe, and the most stunning head. She was so beautiful I felt as if I couldn't move. All I could do was stare in radiant wonder, marveling how such a lovely pony could have even existed. A girl walked into the indoor with a halter.

"Is that Phoenix?" I managed to stammer.

"This pony?" the girl said. "No, this is my pony, Tommy Girl."

"Oh," I said, slightly let down.

"There's Phoenix, over in the corner stall," the girl replied, and left with her pony trailing behind. I looked into the corner stall.

Bam! The door slammed behind my mom as she came in with the lady who was showing us the pony.

"Hi! I'm Carrie," the lady said. "I'll go and grab Phoenix now; why don't you guys go wait in the barn? It's heated."

That was enough for me! I went straight to the barn. I talked with the girl who owned Tommy Girl for a while, then I heard mom and Carrie come in.

"L.R.," Carrie said, "This is Phoenix."

Phoenix was ... interesting. Her head was definitely not the nicest; in fact, she looked more like Jekyll and Hyde, because while one side of her face looked ... not bad, the other was almost all white with a big watch eye to match. She had okay conformation ... well not really. She looked more like a huge muscle that happened to have a head attached. Her butt could have been mistaken for Europe, because it was so big. I also noticed her pinning her ears and rolling her eyes at Carrie and my mom.

"What's up with that?" I asked.

"Phoenix has high standards for whom she likes and doesn't like," Carrie replied, bopping Phoenix on the nose for trying to bite her.

Phoenix seemed to like me. At least she wasn't trying to bite me, which was a step in the right direction. She pinned her ears as I tightened her girth, and there were a few moments when she looked at me and I thought smoke might come out of her nose, and her eyes might turn blood red. She also looked a bit carnivorous when she tried to eat my mom's shoulder in the halter-to-bridle crossover change. I tried to hide a snicker as I looked at my mom, who obviously was not amused. I could tell she wasn't fond of this pony at all.

But I, on the other hand, thought Phoenix was fabulous! I loved her spunky, street-punk-type attitude. Every time she tried to bite someone, she looked at me as if to say,"Hey! High-five me on that! She'll have a bruise for weeks!"

As I walked by my mom, I mouthed, "Isn't she absolutely fabulous!?"

"Oh yeah. Just what a beginning 5-year-old short stirrup kid could cuddle and hug. Unless, that is, she bit her neck first!" mom replied.

I walked Phoenix up to the mounting block. She stood stock still. I looked at my mom as if trying to say, "See ... She's really quiet!" with my eyes.

I gathered up the reins and some mane in my left hand, put my right hand on the pommel, and put my left foot in the stirrup. As I was about to swing my leg over, Phoenix reared, and took off crow hopping and bucking around the indoor. Then she suddenly stopped, but before I could do anything, she bolted. I thought I might stay on if

I threw my leg over her side, but Phoenix had other plans. She stopped dead. I think I must've ended up somewhere on her head, which she ever-so-politely threw back, sending me off with a one-way ticket to the ground.

Both Mom and Carrie looked at me, not quite knowing what to do. I helped them out—by laughing. Carrie looked puzzled and said, "There's only one kid I know who would go through all that, and end up laughing, and believe me, L.R., you have no competition!"

My mom just sort of laughed and shook her head. I turned around to see Phoenix's mouth right in my face. She seemed to be saying, "Gotcha! I told you I'm naughty!"

I laughed, dusting myself off.

I pulled the reins over her head and walked to the mounting block for the second time. Phoenix stood still again. Instead of taking my sweet time again, I got on much faster. Phoenix reared again. I kicked her. She bucked and was about to take off, but then stopped, almost stunned. She turned her head and looked at me, and I saw the evil smirk in her big watch eye.

"We're gonna get along fine, j-u-s-t f-i-n-e," she seemed to be saying in a sly, sneering kind of way. She was right.

The rest of the trial went the same way. Phoenix pulled every trick in the book: bucked, bolted, scooted, you name it. But as we began jumping her, we noticed something. Phoenix had a jump that was simply phenomenal!

"Could we raise the fence a little bit, Carrie?" Mom asked. Carrie nodded.

The triple bar was now at about three-feet-six inches. I took a deep breath (to this day, I swear Phoenix did the same), and we headed toward the fence. I tried not to feel nervous because I knew if I showed any fear, I would end up eating wood poles. I could feel Phoenix start to head over the fence. It was amazing! She simply flew over it as if it were a crossrail. It felt perfect. She wasn't letting me get away with sitting and looking nice, and I wasn't letting her pull any tricks. We were each doing our fair share, not forcing one to do more then the other. This is why I think we get along so well. We're the yin-yang theory: She makes up for what I don't have, and I make up for what she doesn't have.

We did the fence a few more times. Then Mom and I drove away to look at another pony. After we had driven for a little bit, Mom asked me which pony was my favorite so far. I looked at her and replied, simply, "Phoenix."

My mom wasn't too keen on the idea at first. She wasn't—and still isn't—sure how on earth she was going to resell this pony, but I told her she never would have to.

It was only February when Phoenix got to Horton's Farm where I train, but it seemed like forever to me. I really wanted her to be waiting at the barn when I got home. My trainer, Joe Forrest, decided (after seeing us together) that we really were a "match made in heaven."

Phoenix and I trained together until April; at that point, show season ran into us like a brick wall. At the first show of the season, we did the pony jumpers and pony hunters. Because it was my first time doing jumpers, I rode a bit too conservatively. Phoenix, however, rose to the challenge, and we earned the reserve championship for our division. I was thrilled.

"You better get used to winning," the gatekeeper told me. "You two are really amazing out there!"

Phoenix and I took that good man's advice! Throughout the season, we dominated the pony jumper divisions, winning champion or reserve champion at nearly every show we went to. We even picked up some decent ribbons in the hunters. At one show, I was called in to jog first for the conformation pony hunter class. And while I was moved down two places due to Phoenix's lack of "correct conformation," I was just as excited as if we had won. Just to be called in first was enough for me!

Since I seem to keep getting taller, this year will probably be my last with Phoenix, but I plan to lease her to another young rider next year. I think what Phoenix has taught me as a rider is important because she made me go back to the basics, and pretty much forced me to use my seat, hands, and legs ... things I sometimes forget about, since I work so hard to look nice. Phoenix has taught me that the rider must give an animal the support it needs. She's also taught me that, as much as I like to "ride pretty," sometimes you've just got to sit up and be effective.

It will be hard for me to let Phoenix go, but I know that what she's taught me will never leave me. So, in a way, Phoenix will never leave or be as far away as I fear. My main hope is that she can go on to teach other children in her future, so by the time she's retired, they'll be a little piece of Phoenix shared by a whole generation of riders. ☺

Lora Rachel ("L.R.") Davidson is a multi-talented 13-year-old who not only exhibits ponies competitively on the "A" circuit, but also has been a professional actress since the age of 10 weeks, appearing with numerous regional theatres and in movies, television shows and commercials. Although she also shows in the hunters and in equitation, L.R. especially loves the jumper divisions—particularly the new pony jumpers, where she has quickly established herself as a top "pony jockey."

Editor's Note: Since the writing of this story, Phoenix has been leased to a young rider in Florida, and continues to showcase her talents on the A show circuit.

Stan

By Amy Habeck

The popular saying, "You can't judge a book by its cover," was defined to me a few years ago. I had recently sold my Arabian horse, "Cody," due to the financial struggles that come with being a newlywed. At the time, I was working at a stable that boarded horses and trained American Saddlebreds. I loved my job there. In fact, the barn owners were like a second family to me.

The year I sold Cody, the barn owners had gone to Illinois to check out a few Saddlebreds that were for sale.

When they returned with "Stan," I couldn't believe my eyes. His head and rear end were clearly visible, but his back was not. Stan had been born with a genetic defect called a "sway back." In addition, he was dirty and had a mane that went in every possible direction.

As it turned out, Stan had been thrown into the trailer as a "freebie." No one else wanted him, and he may have ended up as dog food if he hadn't been brought home to our stable. I have to admit that I laughed along with the others when I first saw how low his back was. He was awkward in every way.

The stable was quite busy during those days, and as a result, nobody had any time to spend with Stan. That is, until the barn owners, knowing that I was still feeling the loss of Cody, decided I needed a new "project." At that moment, Stan and I began our journey together.

Stan was a yearling at the time and had no training whatsoever. I had my work cut out for me. First on the list was a good bath and clipping. The poor horse was covered with dirt and fleas. From then on we worked together every day. After work, I turned him out into the field with my friend's horse, Precious; they loved to run and kick together.

I was falling in love with Stan more and more each day. However, the other boarders often joked or commented on Stan's sway back. At first these comments hadn't bothered me, but now they did. His imperfection may have been visible to everyone else, but each day it became less and less noticeble to me. I saw a beautiful, jet black horse with two perfectly matched socks on his back legs. His eyes were wide and expressive. He had a big heart and a lot of patience. I had never trained a Saddlebred before, and poor Stan, bless his heart, had to put up with all my mistakes.

After much lungeing and training with a bitting rig and long lines, the day finally came for our first ride together. I was nervous, but Stan handled the situation wonderfully. I slowly placed my right leg over his back and settled into the saddle. With an assistant holding Stan on a lunge line, we began. As we walked around the arena, Stan listened intently to each command and never once bolted. I am sure he was a bit scared too, but I never felt it.

That winter I received a wonderful Christmas gift—Stan. I was thrilled, and my husband supported it 100 percent. I went up to the barn that night and wrapped my arms around Stan's strong black neck, and told him he was mine. It was a moment that I will never forget.

As our training progressed, I set my sights on the following show season. I wanted to get Stan to at least one show. I had to take special care of his back, using special padding so he wouldn't get sore. That summer we entered our first show—a nice, relaxed, schooling show. Not only was this Stan's first show, but mine as well. I was pretty nervous and broke out with hives all over!

When our class was called, we entered the ring along with three other saddleseat riders. I was thrilled when we placed second. With a saddle on, Stan's swayback was not so obvious. And somehow that second place ribbon lessened the hurt I felt from the comments I'd always heard around the barn.

Stan was growing like a weed; by that winter, he was close to 17 hands. His back never improved, but that was no longer a concern of mine. We continued to train, working now toward the double bridle. This was going to be interesting. Stan found out that his new favorite thing was rearing. This was not fun. I am sure this new-found addiction had something to do with me. I was trying to adapt to holding two reins instead of one and probably hit the curb bit a little to hard at first. With a little help from the pros at the stable, we got back on track. Stan still reared, but it was outside during playtime.

Our work schedule became more vigorous as spring approached. Stan got his first set of show shoes. Finally it was time to get back into the ring. We entered a class B Saddlebred show. With Stan in his full bridle, and me dressed in a bright red saddleseat coat, we entered the ring. When the ribbons were given, Stan and I placed second. I thought we did great considering it was a newer and bigger ring then our first show. The spectators also sat on a deck on the rail, which was a bit scary to Stan. We survived, and I was very pleased without performance.

The show that meant the most to me was also our biggest. We entered an English three-gaited class with more than 20 other entries. When Stan arrived that day and I led him off the trailer, I couldn't tell if it was his height or his back that people were looking at. I did hear for the first time, "what a beautiful animal," coming from the barns as we walked by. I smiled and knew in my heart that these people were beginning to see what I had seen a long time ago.

This show was going to be a challenge to us both; we had a lot of good competition. As I placed the saddle on Stan's back, he lowered his head so I could get his bridle on. His black coat glistened in the sun. I put on my red coat, and we were off. I had never felt so tall as I did that day. As his shoes clopped on the pavement, Stan held his head high. I thought to myself that we had done this together. We were both full of pride and couldn't keep it to ourselves.

The horse no one thought was worth a dime placed fourth that day out of 20. When I reached down to receive our ribbon, I knew this was our best day—his and mine. Unfortunately, that would be our last show together. Due to a job change, I knew that I would no longer have the time for Stan.

My friend Les and her horse Precious had moved to a stable in nearby Oshkosh. The trainer at the stable expressed an interest in Stan. Within days, I had to put Stan in a trailer and let him go. I knew I had to do this for him, but it hurt me more than anything I had ever done before. We had learned, worked and played together. We grew through each other's mistakes and victories.

I learned from Stan the meaning of inner beauty and the power to overcome one's shortcomings. Thanks to all the wonderful people who brought him into my life and to God who knew I needed him. I will never forget this wonderful animal and how he touched my soul. I hope, in some way, I enriched his life as well. ☼

Amy Habeck lives in Appleton, Wisconsin. She enjoys art, walking with her dog, Griffin, and spending time with her husband, John. Recently, they purchased their first home and hope to start a family soon. Although Amy does not have a horse at this time, she hopes to become a horse owner again in the future. Amy is thankful to those who brought "Stan" into her life, and to her mom and dad for giving her first pony as a child.

Willow

By Tanya Haught and Peter Vinogradov

A few strokes of my rusty hammer drove the last galvanized nail through a sheet of corrugated tin. The last thump struck the new roofing with a jolt that reverberated through the pasture and sent my four plump Thoroughbreds into yet another agitated stampede. It was a warm, clear Memorial Day that brought students, teachers, and parents from our school together in an effort to put the finishing touch on a quarantine barn for two horses whose names we did not yet know.

The project had been the culmination of numerous bake sales, e-mails, and phone calls orchestrated by a handful of dedicated students who wanted to make a difference in the fight against horse abuse and neglect. For weeks, donations of material, time and money had passed through the hands of our little equine rescue class. And as we all stood back to admire the two-stall barn we had erected, we could begin to picture the two lucky animals that would soon call it home. For me, it was an emaciated Thoroughbred, possibly four years old, off the racetrack with a long list of bruises, sprains and memories of harsh handlers. For others it was a starving foal, just rescued from the hidden shack of a farmer with a tight fist and a heart with no compassion.

We held on to these images, and even shared a few as the drills and hammers were put away in toolboxes, all of us unaware that it would be several weeks before those stalls played host to anything. The money from our candy sales and other donations had already been wired to a carefully chosen horse rescue outfit called Carpe Diem. I had been in touch, several times, with the founder of that organization and knew she was in a hurry to get us our horses.

From her slight German accent, I had imagined

Anja to be a heavy-set, middle-aged woman who could make the most of those funds and find the ideal horses for us to foster. She had braved the barns and auction pens at New Holland many times before, had seen the horses as they went, one by one, into mercenary hands that would eventually push them into double-decked trailers and haul them away to a slow death in a cold slaughterhouse. I had no doubt, therefore, that she would use our money well, would pick out a worthy horse for us to nurture back to health and eventually place in a secure home.

We had agreed that whatever horses she bought would be trailered up to our farm on the day of the auction, one day after our Memorial Day barn raising. So when that day arrived, I was filled with an anxious anticipation that I could only settle by making last-minute adjustments to the stalls, laying out the perfect amount of bedding and preparing a battery of ointments and dietary supplements with which to heal my new charges. By that afternoon, I found myself waiting on the couch, staring past the gravel driveway and trying to calculate how long it could possibly take for Anja to drive a trailer from New Holland to my front door.

By nightfall, I was frantic, wondering if this woman,

whom I had never actually met, would ever arrive, or whether I had unwittingly made myself the manager of the most disastrous community project in our school's history. Anja's phone call at 7:00 the next morning relieved my anxiety somewhat, until she began to tell me what had occurred at the auction.

With the students' earnings, she had rescued two horses. One was a Thoroughbred gelding whose leg was so badly damaged that he could not endure more than an hour of trailering at a time. The other was a severely underweight old mare. The gelding's leg made transport upstate virtually impossible, and Anja sadly reported that he would have to stay at a foster home farther south until he was sound enough to travel (which, according to the vet, might well have been never). The students' money and effort, she reminded me, had met their objective. I was overcome, however, with a guilty sense of heartbreak in knowing that those kids, who would soon be gone on summer vacations, might never see tangible proof of their accomplishment.

And I began to wonder, as I contemplated the empty two-stall barn, why Anja had chosen as she did. Wasn't New Holland the equine equivalent of a battlefield? Didn't it make sense to save a horse that at least stood a decent chance of recovery, or one that at least had a few years left in her to enjoy that recovery? The shame of that sort of thinking hit me at once, but having never met the two horses Anja rescued, I could not keep myself from thinking that they held two tickets to happiness that they might never get to use.

In the weeks that followed, my worries faded as I began to receive e-mailed photos of the horses, accompanied by regular progress reports from Anja. She had developed a sweet spot for the gelding and had given him the name "Barak." The few girls from our horse-rescue class who had not left for the summer chose the name "Willow" for the mare that had been rescued with him.

It was late June before the pair finally arrived, driven in an old red trailer supplied by one of Anja's many accomplices. Anja's own appearance surprised me. She was neither heavy-set nor middle-aged, but rather young, somewhat shy, and thin. And as slight and unobvious as she was, her charges, the two rescued horses, were even slighter, and as I watched them wobble off the trailer on their hay-stalk legs, I marveled at how such frames could continue to support life.

Willow was the first out of the trailer, and she made

the descent with a mere stumble. Barak, with his injured leg, took several minutes to ease himself down and required all of our goading and reassurance. We helped the pair to their new pasture, introduced them to their new stalls, and turned them about several times as Anja pointed out the long list of skin lesions, hoof injuries, scrapes, and swellings. As it was late in the day, Anja was anxious to be on the road. She left a few minutes later with many words of thanks and wishes of good luck.

My own plump Thoroughbreds were all fascinated by the new arrivals, particularly by Barak, who was the closest thing to a stallion any of them had seen in years. Within minutes of Anja's departure, my horses had either vaulted or destroyed the plastic quarantine fence that we had erected, and now stood with their necks craned over the more sturdy wooden fence hoping to get a closer sniff.

The days that followed were hot ones, the kind that dry up water buckets faster than horses can drink, and that kill grass in minutes, leaving nothing but dust to settle onto sweaty backs. For the most part, I ignored the heat, being so utterly absorbed, as I was, with getting food into the two skeletons in my back pasture. I hosed all of the animals at least three times a day, in spite of the fact that local officials had begun asking residents to conserve water. At night, I tucked everyone in, spending at least an hour in each of the rescue stalls just to make sure Willow and Barak were getting comfortable.

Barak was emaciated, and his legs were extremely stiff and shaky, but I could tell that he was a beautiful horse. As I looked at Willow, it seemed that every area on her body that could sink was sunken. She was still wearing a shoe when Carpe Diem found her at New Holland, and I suspect she worked right up until she was brought to auction. Her teeth were worn to near nubs, and many were missing. The vet later said that the excessive wear was probably a result of years spent eating dirt, as many chronically undernourished horses are known to do. She was profoundly shy, and while she let us pet her and brush her, she did so with a terrified resignation. Nonetheless, they both seemed to be surviving, and I felt it would be only a few months before the two were as fat and healthy as my others were.

Therefore, when Willow stopped eating one morning, therefore, I wanted to hope that she was merely fatigued from the sun. When she managed to achieve an almost dog-like pant later in the day, I knew we were not so fortunate. I could find no cause for her distress, but the vet had better luck. She managed to extract from Willow's hoof a slender shaft of rusted metal that might have once been a nail or a bit of barbed wire. It had been buried in her hoof so long that the frog had actually grown over top of it.

The weeks that followed became what I felt would be Willow's last struggle. The daily antibiotic shots sent her into a motionless stupor. Having not eaten for days, she soon gave up on water as well, and her skeletal frame began to shrink even more. I hosed her down constantly for fear of the heat, wiped her brow with a wet sponge every five minutes, and began sitting in her stall all night just to watch her chest rise and fall. It was then that I realized how little it mattered how old this animal was, or how lame, or how toothless, or how seemingly beyond repair. What did it matter that a younger, healthier mare might have been saved? This was the one we got, and this was the one who needed our love. I began to wonder, as I examined the lumps on her face, her bare gums and her fallen hooves, whether Willow had known a day of happiness in her many long years. Had she ever been sponged on a hot day? Would her life of misery end with nothing but antibiotics and a persistent heat wave?

It didn't help my conscience to note how Willow took everything with unflagging patience. She'd obviously been hit many times before, and how on earth could she tell that our poking her with needles and shoving syringes full of water down her throat weren't just more abuse? Somehow, she did, and somehow she tolerated it all.

Another vet came to see Willow several days after the first. He lightened her antibiotics, gave us a bunch of pastes designed to jump start her digestive system, and told us we might want to start thinking about where to bury her. It killed me to think that Willow might die having known nothing but suffering. After another day of forcing Gatorade and water down her throat, we sat in her stall as she lay there breathing softly. We stayed up until 3a.m. with her, telling her stories about what her happy day would be like, how she'd eat 'til she couldn't stand it, how she'd be the fattest horse in the pasture, and how Barak would make her his girlfriend because she looked so pretty.

Willow recovered almost as swiftly as she had taken ill. The new treatments, the Gatorade, and our promises for a better life seemed to do it for her and before too long she began slurping down her watery senior feed mush like it was carrot sauce. To this day she has not stopped eating. Her broken teeth and hardened gums have become an efficient team. Her skin has cleared up, and is now covered with the softest fur of any horse. Barak hasn't made her his girlfriend yet, and she's still not the fattest mare on the farm, but in the end I don't think that's what she wanted out of life. She seems content to be Barak's vision-impaired playmate, an occasional grandmother to our yearling, and a reminder that no creature, no matter how old or how lame, is beyond compassion.

Tanya Haught and Peter Vinogradov live in Staatsburg, New York. They both work at Poughkeepsie Day School where Tanya teaches biology and Peter teaches foreign languages. For the past two years, they have been inspired by and have contributed to the efforts of Carpe Diem Equine Rescue, an organization dedicated to saving abused and neglected equines.

Mirabelle

By Max Gahwyler, MD

One afternoon, our young veterinarian arrived in our driveway with a trailer behind his truck. Since we had no problems with our horses at the time, we wondered what this was all about. We very quickly learned.

In a court decision that very morning, a few horses and ponies had been removed from their owner as they had been terribly neglected and all but abandoned. Our vet, knowing that we had an empty stall, apologized and asked if we could accommodate a small pony for a short time.

This pony was in such bad shape that she wasn't expected to live for very long.

As the pony was led out of the trailer, we saw something that looked more like a skinny goat—filthy, and with a sad, abandoned look, but too weak to show any other reaction. We quickly prepared the box stall for the mare and led her inside. The vet put her on IV saline and glucose and we fed her a small supper of soaked pellets and mash; she stayed on this regime for a week. As she began to gain a bit of strength, we had her dewormed and her teeth floated. When our blacksmith came, we had her feet trimmed. After a week, we put her out into the paddock with our other horses, and she quickly became attached to my Prinz. Gradually, her food intake was increased and, as she gained weight, she began to look more and more like a cute little woolly Shetland pony.

Still, this pony had a constant worried, questioning look as if she wanted to tell us something. One day, we decided to call Penelope Smith, an animal communicator with whom we had consulted in the past. We hoped that Penelope would be able to tell us more about our new boarder.

As it turned out, Penelope was able to find out a lot about Mirabelle's past. She had been used for children's pony rides and country fairs. In between, she had been turned out alongside other horses that kept her from the sparse hay that was thrown into the paddock. Even when she foundered, she had to work. Her biggest concern was what we expected of her in return for all of the care we had given her.

Penelope communicated to her that we did not expect anything of her, and that she could finally relax and enjoy her remaining years. Even so, she did not quite seem to believe it. Then, one day after I had completed my ride on Prinz, we put Mirabelle on a leadline and, as I cooled out my big boy Prinz, ponied her around the polo field, first at a slow walk and later at a bit of trot.

Mirabelle was approximately 34 years old when she arrived at our farm, and against all expectations, remained with us for 10 more happy years. To this day, her name plate remains on the stall door. ♘

Silver,
The "Houdini" Horse

By Terry Boaz

We never knew what type of entertainment Silver had planned for us. On occasion it would be a moonlight saunter. It is a startling experience to be awakened in the wee hours of the morning by a horse—especially when he has chosen to stroll through the middle of a modern mobile home park. It is embarrassing to retrieve one's overly friendly horse while in one's pajamas, or to find him happily rolling on a neighbor's front lawn. Try to explain to someone that your horse has cleverly crawled under his fence. Horses don't usually do that sort of thing, but Silver did.

Some joked that Silver was "Houdini" reincarnated. No horse could pick a gate latch as quickly or master a maze of obstacles meant to deter his escape as effortlessly as he did. I watched him nonchalantly push, pry and poke his way out of his stall, then walk slowly over to his paddock gate, take the latch in his teeth, spit it out and give the gate a shove with his pink nose. Thus Silver earned the nickname, "Houdini Horse".

True to the Houdini reputation, Silver had many unnerving tricks. He could make a brush, rake, halter— anything—disappear right before your very eyes. One minute I saw it, the next minute it vanished! But there is Silver innocently batting his baby blues at me wondering why I was so upset.

I would find objects in the most surprising places— brushes at the bottom of horse troughs, blankets buried beneath sawdust, hammers pulled halfway through walls and the water hose in the middle of the corral ... watering dust instead of the trough. But all of this made Silver what he was, a lovable clown at heart.

One August day in 1972, I was sitting on a stump

near Silver's stall and was joined by a couple of kids who also boarded horses there. I was worrying about a dream that I had about a barn fire. There had been several unexplained barn fires in our area recently. Soon we were discussing what would happen to Silver if his barn caught fire. Could Houdini Horse get out of it, or would he return to his flaming home as many horses do?

Shortly afterward I led an old bay mare out of the barn into the pasture, leaving Silver the only horse left in the weary building. I just felt uneasy leaving the mare in the barn and felt young Silver was better prepared to take care of himself. I felt foolish about my fears as I threw Silver a flake of alfalfa and walked home.

"FIRE!" The call rang thunderously through the night. I leaped up from bed. My husband yelled, "The barn's on fire! Silver!"

My heart sank as I saw the barn erupt into a wall of flames, raging and leaping like a giant torch. I jumped into some clothes and followed my husband out the back door. The flames were climbing higher, illuminating the area like the bright sun. The heat was so intense that it could be felt over 100 yards away.

From the corner of my eye I saw the frail frame of

the old mare making her way to safety on a slope far behind the barn. Fate had chosen her path. It was ironic that she, who had been blessed with more than 20 years, should live to see more. Had my Silver gone in her place?

Shouts echoed through the air. "Turn the hoses on your trailers!" shouted someone from the mobile home park.

"Help! It's leaping up the fence!" came a cry from my left.

"Oh! That poor white horse was in there!" cried another, "Did anyone get him?"

My husband ran to wake the widow who lived in the farmhouse. They appeared in shadowy forms dragging a hose toward the fire. A huge tree towered above the barn. If it caught, more than Silver would be lost! It would rage relentlessly through the dry surroundings. It was up to us to contain the fire until the fire department arrived. We were not alone in our fight—soon friends, neighbors and even strangers came to our aid.

A distant cry pierced the night above the crackling of the flames. It was shrill and eerie. I whirled around to see a ghost drift across the far end of the pasture. Dazed, I could not believe my eyes. It was a horse running wildly across the bottom of the pasture. Then he raised his head to look at me. It was not until he galloped toward me that I realized that it was my horse! Silver was alive! I threw my arms around his lathered neck and buried my face in his mane.

Soon it was all over. The firemen were hosing down the remains of Silver's home. Everyone shook their heads in disbelief—the paddock fence still stood intact, attached to the smoldering ruins. Silver had cleared a four-foot fence from a standstill to gain his freedom. That night he truly earned his nickname of "Houdini Horse!" The old barn was gone, but nothing in the form of life had perished.

Now and then, men and animals are gifted with a special courage to see them through an ordeal that is beyond normal strength. Silver received such a gift when he was given the ability to jump the fence and the good sense to get away from the fire.

Our half-Mustang registered American Creme Albino, Silver Chico, better known as Houdini Horse, happily roamed a beautiful pasture in the foothills of the Sierra Nevada Mountains until the ripe old age of 33. For the remainder of his days he enjoyed the sweet spring water and the company of an albino mare. No more barns—he earned the right to run free. ♘

Terry Boaz resides in the California Sierra Nevada foothills with her husband, Lowell, and son, Tim. She has owned and trained horses for 30 years. Terry also raises and trains AKC German Shepherds. As a hobby, she writes articles and animal stories which have been published in various horse and animal magazines, along with her original artwork.

Mine 'Orse

By Marianne Alexander

Matthew and his family came to visit Greystone Farm in 1993. He was only five years old, but very much wanted to have his own pony. Matthew referred to all of the ponies at Greystone as "Mine 'Orse." He could not understand why one of them could not get into the car and go home with him.

Matthew has Down's Syndrome. At the time of his visit, Personal Ponies did not have a pony for him. He had to wait another year, until a foal might be born who could grow up and become Matthew's very own "Mine 'Orse."

In the summer of 1995, a tiny yellow colt was born on a nearby breeder's farm. The call went out to Matthew's family; Mine 'Orse" was waiting. Again, Matthew was so excited that he couldn't understand why the pony couldn't come home in the car with him. He had to wait until the tiny foal could be weaned; then, it would become his very own pony.

It was a long summer for Matthew. He visited his little "'Orse" nearly every weekend. He learned how to brush him and how to put his halter on. Matthew's little "'Orse" was named Blue Star, but Matthew insisted the pony's real name was "Mine 'Orse." Nobody argued with that!

One day when Matthew came home from school, there in his front yard was his dearly loved "Mine 'Orse" standing on the lawn. Matthew just stared and stared and stared. It had been a long time to wait for his pony;. Matthew was now seven years old.

Matthew has a chair in the corner of his pony's stall, and when Matthew sits down in the chair, his little pony trots over and puts his head against Matthew's chest. Matthew then scratches Star's ears, and they are a very happy pair. Matthew's physical skills have improved since the pony entered his life. He can clean Star's stall with his little shovel; of course he needs help, but he is learning. He has learned how to carry hay and water to his pony without spilling it. He enjoys these tasks and has grown more responsible.

Matthew and his mom read bedtime stories in "Mine 'Orse's" stall, and Matthew's mother tells us that the entire family has become closer since a miniature Shetland pony came to live with them.

And best of all, there is a love affair between a little boy with Down's Syndrome and a tiny yellow pony. ♘

A horse! A horse!
My kingdom for a horse!

William Shakespeare,
Richard III

Babe

By Shannon Rogers

Babe was the one who started it all. I guess you could say she was the beginning of a lifelong obsession. Though I have ridden and owned many horses since, there has never been one who has touched that special place in my heart like she did.

It is strange how some things become locked in our memories, just as if they happened a moment ago ... a frozen frame for us to look back upon. I can't remember what I just went into the kitchen to get, but I can remember the first time I saw Babe. It is still as clear as a bell.

I was a ripe 4 years old—4½ to be precise. We—my parents, my brother and I—were at my grandparents' house. This was nothing unusual, as my Dad and Grandad ran the ranch together. But this day was to be something special: I was getting a new horse.

I remember being terrified and, at the same time, being so excited that it seemed like every moment was an eternity. Neither Mom nor Grandmother had seen the horse yet, so when the trailer pulled in and the horse was unloaded, it was something of a shock for us all. My father was beaming, my grandfather was dubious—though in truth it was he who was responsible for getting this horse.

The gate to the trailer swung open and out backed the largest horse I had ever seen. I don't really remember much about that moment other than a shocked, "Good grief, James Harry! She's huge!" from my mom. Mom absolutely never spoke in that tone of voice, which is probably why I remember it so well.

Dad simply ignored her comment and proudly led the horse over to me. "Her name's Babe," he said. I remember gazing up into his proud eyes, then craning my neck so far back it hurt, just to get a look at this horse's face. With an uncanny ability that I would later learn was second nature to her, Babe seemed to understand the problem.

Down, down, down came her head. Her head was huge. She was huge. I think I must have been born loving horses because surely if I had not, I would have run screaming in the other direction.

The first thing I noticed when she put her head down was the funny white streak that ran down it. Then I met her eyes—those beautiful brown eyes. They were not ordinary horse eyes; these were the eyes of something else. They had all kinds of emotions in them and were incredibly gentle. Babe's eyes told me that I could trust her to take care of me. They did not lie, I could and I did. I fell completely in love right there on the spot.

Mom, on the other hand, with fresh pictures of me flying through the air and landing in a feeder, was not so easily convinced. She had never really been around horses, and this was the largest horse she had ever seen up close. She was not about to let her baby get on that animal. And so, one of the few arguments between my parents ensued.

Babe didn't care, and I didn't care. She was MY horse; Daddy had said so. I stood there rubbing her nose and talking to her, completely ignoring what was going on around me.

Daddy related to Mom all the reasons why Babe was such a perfect horse for me. (It didn't seem to matter that I could walk beneath her without bending over much). Babe had been owned by one man for most of her 16 years. She was an registered Appendix Quarter Horse, and all the Thoroughbred showed, in her size, her frame and everywhere else. The man who had owned her had been a professional rodeo rider; Babe had roped at Madison Square Garden more than once. Then, later on, when the man formed his own rodeo stock contracting business, Babe had led the parades and the grand entry to the rodeos.

While Mom wasn't totally convinced, it was decided that I would be allowed to ride her. And so, my tiny child's saddle was strapped to her huge back, and I was boosted aloft. I had never been so far above the ground! I remember thinking how neat it was that I was above so many of the oak limbs, and that I could see over the top of the pickup. Away we went in a very stately walk. I had been ordered to stay in the general vicinity, so we made a loop, very slowly, my feet sticking straight out from her sides.

Everything was fine. Then I remember hearing a helicopter—not unusual, as Ft. Hood was close by. Grandad always let the Army hold their maneuvers on his property.

The helicopter noise got louder and louder and louder, and to my surprise, the helicopter landed between 50 and 80 yards from Babe and me. It seemed this was the weekend of the maneuvers, and everyone but the Army had forgotten about it.

Babe stopped walking and stood there looking at the helicopter. I remember a man getting out of the chopper and coming over to us. He appeared very jolly, as though the entire episode of landing a chopper that close to a horse with a child on it was funny. He walked right up to Babe and me and offered to let me ride in the helicopter if I would let him ride Babe. It was probably the most flatly refused offer he ever got.

I don't remember the rest of that day, but Babe became a trusted member of the family after that. I guess Mom figured that Babe had withstood the test of fire and passed. I was allowed to freely roam on her wherever my heart desired , be it across the street to the huge park or on the 70 acres behind the house. If I thought I was big enough to do it, Babe took me there and protected me all the way. She also had more sense than I did. If she thought it was a little much she would turn us around, regardless of what I told her to do, and march us straight home.

I learned to ride bareback on her; I had to. Even standing on a barrel up ended didn't launch me high enough to put the saddle on her back. Bless her, she never complained. I might also add that if Babe hadn't wanted to be ridden, there would have been no way in the world that I could have gotten the bridle on her. She always put her dear head down so that I could reach her.

My little brother walked back and forth underneath her stomach; she never so much as moved an eyelash. He swung from her tail; she did not care. He climbed all over her as though she were a jungle gym; she never moved a muscle.

I rode Babe everywhere. She was my best friend, and I loved her with all my soul and might. Babe never once let me down during those eight years.

Then came a time of change. Dad had been hurt while gathering cattle, and the bottom fell out of the market. The next year it was announced that he was getting out of ranching and going back into banking. We were moving to Amarillo, and our beloved Babe could not come with us. I cannot begin to describe the emotions that still rage in me over that decision and separation. I felt as though a part of me had been torn loose, never to return.

A good home was found for her though, with twin girls whom I dare say loved her as much as we did. I know they did; their whole family did. When they bought her, it was with the understanding that it was for life, and if anything changed we were to get her back. They kept their word.

Six years later, their father called Mom. He said, and I quote from what my mother told me, "Ann, I called to tell you that Babe died. She didn't suffer. She simply lay down under her tree in her paddock and went to sleep. I checked on her that morning when I fed her and she was fine. When I got home that evening she was gone. Ann, my father passed away this past year and you know, I never cried. I cried when Babe died."

Indeed, they both cried on the phone together as they shared the memories of their girls growing up, and a magnificent bay mare helping them along.

What finer tribute could there possibly be? ⚘

Shannon Rogers still loves to ride and has passed that love on to her daughter. She teaches school in Ft. Worth, Texas and is the author of three fantasy novels. You can read more about Shannon and her horses by visiting her website at:
www.geocities/com/Heartland/Park/5848.

The Reiver

By Sandy Sternberg

The Reiver, a chestnut gelding, was originally purchased as a two-year-old at an auction house in Edison, New Jersey. The purchase price was $40. The horse was so thin and covered with sores that not even the "killers" were interested in him. The gal who bought Reiver, Maureen Mack, did so simply to save him from more pain and suffering. She never even got on his back.

With love and sustenance, Maureen nursed Reiver back to health. She then sold him to a nice young girl, Sue

Rossi, who with the help of her trainer, slowly brought him to the hunter world. We ended up buying him for one of my students, Wendy, when he was jumping a bit.

This was not the first time I had seen Reiver. I had looked at him six months earlier, when searching for a horse for another student. However, Reiver and this first student did not get along well. In fact, he ran away with the child, and I literally had to step in front of him to stop him. This horse had spirit, but was not about to put up with a bouncy beginner. When I grabbed the reins, shouting, "sit back," to the student, Reiver circled to a stop with the most surprised look on his face.

I don't know why, but I kept thinking about him, and when Wendy decided to purchase a horse, I returned to visit the spirited chestnut.

Of course, I was a lot more cautious this time, and rode him before allowing the student on his back. The Reiver was a saint for me, and Wendy got along with him as well. He kept looking at me, and I found myself wondering if he remembered the "crazy lady" who stepped in front of him and brought him to a screeching halt.

Wendy's parents purchased the horse and brought him back to Pepperhill Farm. The following day, Wendy had her first lesson with Reiver. In fact, Wendy's Mom had even come out to watch the new couple in action. In those days, our establishment was very small and space was quite limited. Our outside course shared a 4'6" fence with the riding ring. Wendy was supposed to jump a line of verticals and halt at the end, just in front of the fence.

Well, Wendy had a habit of leaning forward all the time, even when asking her horse to halt. As she prepared to halt before the fence—leaning forward—Reiver misinterpreted her aids. He thought her leaning forward meant "jump," so while Mom stared in horror, over 4'6" he went, right into the ring. Wendy landed completely out of the saddle, on the horse's neck. I went running over, calming the horse while holding the reins so that Wendy could regain her position. The horse never moved, but kind of gave me the same "look" as he had before, and I just burst into laughter. He certainly did remember me!

The Reiver and Wendy went on to win many three-foot Children's Hunter classes and championships. They showed mostly in New Jersey, including at some of the "A" shows. When Wendy went off to college, she decided she didn't have enough time to ride and asked us to sell Reiver for her.

At this point, my daughter Jill's horse was getting a month-long winter letdown, so Jill and I shared in keeping Reiver fit and ready to sell. Since Jill seemed to get along well with him, we decided to start showing Reiver in an effort to increase his chances of being sold. As luck would have it, we were so happy with his attitude that Jill continued to show him in the Medal and Maclay classes, and Reiver didn't seem to care about the height at all. (Of course, I remembered that 4'6" jump on the outside course with Wendy!)

To make a long story a bit shorter, we purchased the horse from Wendy, and Reiver successfully showed in the Maclay Finals at Madison Square Garden. It was Jill's first time qualifying (at age 15) and Reiver's first time in New York as well. They rode well enough to be invited back to test in the afternoon, one of 20 or so out of over 150 who had originally qualified.

Wendy's family, who had since relocated, flew in from the mid-west to witness his first time in the Garden. Maureen, the woman who originally rescued Reiver, also came to watch, along with Sue Rossi, the girl from whom Wendy had bought him—all with tears in their eyes, cheering for Jill and Reiver.

Jill and Reiver went on to compete successfully at many other "A" shows, including the prestigious USET Young Riders Medal Finals at Gladstone, New Jersey. After Jill moved out of the junior ranks, Reiver guided two other students to the Medal and Maclay Finals.

I still have the photos of Reiver as a two-year-old. They send a shiver down my spine every time I see how anorexic he looked and to think about how far he came because he was too thin to "make it" to the killers. I knew I could never sell him and risk having his last days be like his beginning, so we eventually retired The Reiver and he died at Pepperhill Farm at the age of 32. He was truly a one-in-a-million horse. ♻

Sandy Sternberg holds her AHSA registered "R" judge's license in hunters, hunt seat equitation and jumpers. She is also licensed to judge by the International Side-Saddle Organization (ISSO). Sandy has coached her students, both juniors and adults, to wins and championships at major horse shows including Lake Placid, Harrisburg's Pennsylvania National, Grand Pony Hunter Champion at Devon and Champion Small Pony at the Washington International.

The Miracle Foals

By Sara Panjian

It all started the second week of December, 1998. The barn bustled with excitement as the veterinary specialist checked Whitney over. "She is pregnant with twins," the vet said. Of course, we all know few sets of twins ever make it when they are born, and fewer make it four months into the pregnancy. So they did the logical thing, try to pinch one, allowing the other foal to take over and be healthy. Everyone was extremely upset. A couple of weeks later, the vet came back, hoping to find only one twin.

Unfortunately there were still two. So again they tried, but again failed. By then it was too late to go inside the mare and force one to prevail.

That vet, as well as two others, said the mare would lose one or both foals by four months. Four months went by, and the mare showed no signs of losing the foals. The next seven months and two weeks dragged on. Each day the mare seemed to get bigger.

Around the last week of December, one of the other vets came by to give shots and examine Whitney. He predicted that one foal was still alive while the other one had died.

We were all heartbroken, but Dee, the owner, still had hope. She knew there were still two live foals inside of Whitney. Each hour the rest of that week felt like a month. Finally Whitney showed definite signs of foaling.

January 6, 2000 was Whitney's due date. I went to bed around 9:30pm and awoke to my mother at half-past midnight. She exclaimed, "Whitney foaled!" I jumped out of the covers and got dressed a mile a minute and rushed downstairs as my mother and I ran out to the car. Soon after, we were standing in the barn aisle way at the entrance to Whitney's stall. There were two tiny foals lying in there.

They were paints, buckskin and white, with almost identical markings. They each weighed about 50 pounds and were adorable. The filly was the first born and was the smaller, and stronger, of the two. The colt was a little bit clumsy and had a hard time getting up at first.

The next day I stayed at the barn most of the day and watched the vet check the foals and take blood samples back to the lab. When I saw Bam-Bam, the colt, the next day, he was lying on a massive pile of blankets in front of the heater. He was connected to IV and had about a dozen people crowded around him. Evidently he had been dehydrated and had an infection in one of his kidneys. The vet was giving Dee specific instructions on how to turn him over every hour and how to hook up the second bag of IV fluids if he needed it.

The vet didn't really expect the young colt to make it, but a couple of other people who worked at the barn and I were determined to nurse him back to health. When it was time to turn the foal over and reconnect the IV, Dee tried patiently to disconnect the tubing. Several others of us also tried. The connector was stuck. The heater had evidently caused the plastic to expand. At last the connector gave way, but broke doing it. Now we were stuck with a broken IV and a sick foal. Dee called the vet's office and Dee's mother and a boarder went on the 45-minute round trip to Granby to get a new IV system. While they were gone, we bottle fed him, changed his sheets, and babied him. Then he made an attempt to get up. We helped him to his feet, and he romped around the tack room. He was 100 percent better than when I saw him that morning. I was so excited; we all were. Then we fed him and let him take a nap.

When he woke up, he was hungry and full of energy, so we steered him back to the stall with his mother and his sister, Pebbles. When they returned with the IV, we hooked him up again but not for long; he didn't want it anymore. So once again, we brought him back to his stall, and he nursed and hopped around with his sister Pebbles was kind enough to remove the needle from his neck for us.

He is now almost 100 percent better and runs, jumps around and acts almost as energetic as his sister. This is definitely a miracle; two miracle foals, and their mother, Whitney. They have proved statistics and professionals wrong and are doing great. They are the first live set of twins that Connecticut has seen in over 13 years. ♘

Reprinted with the kind permission of **The Horsemen's Yankee Pedlar** and Dee Collier.

No hour of life is lost
that is spent in the saddle.

Winston Churchill

Gidget

By Susanne Aulisio

as told to Kimberly Gatto

It was feeding time on a warm May afternoon when I first noticed that something was wrong. Abu, my Appaloosa, inhaled his grain in typical fashion, but my Quarter Horse, Gidget, seemed to be struggling. In fact, she appeared to be chewing only on one side. As I approached her from the left, I realized that one side of her face was drooping, her ear was not moving, and her eye was not blinking.

Alarmed, I ran up to our house and asked my parents to come outside and look at her. All three agreed that we'd better call the vet. Upon examination, the vet noticed a small bump on Gidget's left eye. Suspecting an infection, he gave us antibiotics to try, but as the days passed, Gidget's condition failed to improve. In fact, the lump seemed to be growing larger.

We called the vet back for another visit. We also consulted with a few specialists. After ruling out the possibility of cancer, one of the vets determined the cause of Gidget's discomfort. It appeared that she had suffered a stroke. Normally, horses' eyes are kept lubricated when they blink, but since she could not do so, the eye had become ulcerated. As a result, Gidget had lost all sight in that eye.

I wasn't aware that strokes could affect horses, and young ones at that. After all, Gidget was only seven years old. She was young and energetic, and loved her daily frolics in the paddock with Abu. Would she survive without the use of her left side? Would she be able to adjust to being blind in one eye? Fear and sadness washed over me as I waited for the vet's prognosis.

Gidget had been a gift from my parents for my ninth birthday. I can still remember waking up that morning, wondering what special gift I would receive. As I lay awake in my bed, I thought about the one thing I wanted more than anything in the world—a horse. I excitedly ran downstairs and found a small jewelry box and a card on the kitchen counter.

Inside the box was a magazine picture of a horse. A bit confused, I turned around and saw my mom, dad and sister standing behind me. With a puzzled look on my face, I listened to a chorus of "Happy Birthday." I held up the picture and asked if I was getting a horse. When they replied, "yes," I became ecstatic.

It was shortly thereafter that I first saw Gidget at a farm in Connecticut. She was a shiny chestnut with a flaxen mane and tail. Her tail was bagged because the owners had been showing her in AQHA conformation classes. When they took her tail out of the bag, it was so gorgeous and thick that it dragged on the ground. The owners explained that they were selling Gidget because she lacked the conformation needed to excel in Quarter Horse classes. As they tacked her up, I stroked her face. We brought her to a huge indoor on the edge of a cliff that overlooked some hills.

There were many other horses in the indoor, one of which was a stallion. My instructor, my mom, dad, and I watched as Gidget was lunged. Her gaits were incredible; to me, her canter looked as if she was floating on clouds. After the owners finished lunging, I climbed aboard the pretty mare's back. As we walked around the stallion began acting up and almost got loose. I became frightened as the horse drew nearer and nearer to us, bucking and rearing. But Gidget didn't seem to care at all. Despite the chaos around her, she walked, trotted and cantered like a pro. At that moment I knew she was the horse for me.

We purchased Gidget and she was moved to the farm where I had been taking lessons. As summer approached, we decided to use her in the farm's camp program to offset the cost of board. Things went well at first, but after a few weeks Gidget began to misbehave. Every time someone would get on her, she would rear up. We originally thought that she had become confused by so many different riders, so I began to ride her exclusively. After a few weeks, however, the problem persisted.

Desperate for help, we asked many trainers for advice on fixing the problem. Most told us there was no help; they said that once a horse had developed a rearing habit, it would always rear. Others gave us tricks to try, none of which worked. Then one of the instructors at my barn recommended Lance, a trainer who was interested in working with Gidget. After a few months of training with Lance, the problem went away. However, when Lance moved to Europe, the problem returned. We decided to give Gidget a few years off to grow up. Gidget became a pet, a pasture horse, retired at seven.

That was just fine with me. It didn't matter that I couldn't ride her; Gidget was a treasured friend to both me and Abu. I had dreamed of one day showing her again, and perhaps breeding her when I finished school. But now all of my hopes and dreams for the future came crashing down in a single moment. Some people suggested that perhaps I should think about putting Gidget to sleep, but I wasn't about to give up so easily. While I would never want to see her suffer, I was determined that somehow we could overcome this.

After thoroughly examining Gidget, the vets drained excess fluid from behind her eye. They prescribed a course of antibiotics for the resulting eye infection, and over the next couple of weeks, we had to keep Gidget's eye moist and clean.

We also made some changes in the everyday routine. With Gidget now blind on the left side, we had to take special care not to upset her. The first thing we did was move her to another stall so that she could see Abu. It really bothered her that she could hear and smell him but couldn't see him. When we moved her to the right hand stall, she could see him clearly with her right (seeing) eye and was content.

Each time I approached Gidget from the left, I had to talk to her so that she would know I was there. In time, she learned to sense how close we were by the change in volume of our voices. It was also difficult for her to go from bright sunlight into a dark barn. We kept a fly mask on her because the paralysis made it to hard for her to "flick" her head to keep the bugs away. It was sad for me to watch her move her head back and forth slowly to try and shoo away the bugs rather than being able to move her head swiftly. Since she still had trouble eating, we chopped her hay to make it easier for her to chew.

At this time, I came up with an idea. If Gidget were to get back into physical shape, perhaps her muscles would repair themselves back to their original state. I told my parents that I wanted to begin riding her again. After several weeks of lungeing, the day came when I was able to once again ride my first horse.

It had been nearly four years since anyone had ridden Gidget. I did not know how she would react to my riding her, especially since she could not see out of her left eye. I got on her expecting the worst, but to my surprise, she was wonderful. I continued working with her and even began jumping small crossrails and verticals.

Finally, I asked my trainer to come over. When she arrived, I was walking out of the barn with Gidget tacked up. I mounted and rode around the ring at a walk, trot, and canter. We even trotted a few crossrails. The next day I rode Gidget down the street to my trainer's farm. She did not rear up at all.

Over time, Gidget got most of her movement back. By last summer, she could blink, move her ear, and chew. Every so often she had trouble eating but was fine as long as she took her time. She has now built up the muscles on the left side of her body; they are strong enough that she no longer has trouble swishing the flies away. When riding her, I have had to work hard to reteach her to bend on the left side, and we periodically have visits with the equine chiropractor to help keep her muscles supple.

My mom recently told me how much it meant to her the first time she saw me riding Gidget after the stroke.

Mom had come home from work and saw my dad standing in the kitchen looking out the window, watching us. She could see me trotting along in the riding ring and had to do a "double-take"; originally she had thought I was riding Abu. As Gidget and I began to canter, balanced and rhythmical, my mom thought about all that we had overcome—the rearing problem, the blindness and the stroke. And her eyes were filled with tears of awe as she watched the two of us ride by. ❧

Susanne Aulisio is sixteen years old and has been riding since she was six. She enjoys taking part in eventing, dressage and jumper competitions with Abu (also known as "Obviously Cool") and plans to also show Gidget this year. Susanne hopes to become a veterinarian specializing in chiropractic care and acupuncture.

A horse is a thing of such beauty ... none will tire of looking at him as long as he displays himself in his splendor.

Xenophon, 400 B.C.

HoneyBee

By Connie Kurtz

She never won a race and she never won a ribbon. The only reason we got her was because her owner owed my father some money for hay. Thus, this barely halter broken three-year-old half-Arabian became ours.

The minute I saw those beautiful brown eyes, I was "head over heels" in love with this horse. Despite the fact that I was told not to go near her (as I was only six and she was a bit wild), each day I always brought her a treat. I knew she wouldn't come and get it, so I would leave it for her and back away, and eventually she would come for it. After a few days, she would take the treat from my hand and let me pet her soft nose. That was when our friendship began.

HoneyBee proved too much for my brothers to handle, so we sent her to a neighbor for training. I can still remember when the trainer called and told us to come and visit. The wild look in HoneyBee's eye was gone, and my brothers could easily ride her. Shortly after that visit, HoneyBee came home with us for good.

My brothers rode her; they loved her speed and exuberance. While I was still not allowed to ride her, I never forgot to bring her treats. One day, as I sat on the fence feeding her, I decided that I was going to get on her back; after all, she was right by the fence so it wasn't so hard for me to climb aboard. HoneyBee never moved a muscle. The whole time I sat on her, I tried with all of my might to get her to walk like I had seen my brothers do. She refused to move. So every day for about a week, I would just sit on her and try to make her walk.

Then one day it happened. She finally walked very slowly and carefully all around the paddock. I was overjoyed. The following day, I put her halter on, fashioned reins out of a lead rope and learned how to steer. I soon became bored with just walking and asked her to trot and, to my delight, she did.

As we improved, I set up little obstacle courses in her paddock and endlessly rode through them. One day, I told my mom that I had a surprise for her. I brought her down to HoneyBee's pen and showed her our moves. Needless to say, mom was surprised! I never did get punished for disobeying my mom's orders, although she did gently tell me that I should have spoken with her before riding and that I should not ride the horse outside of the paddock.

I practiced and practiced in the paddock all summer. I really wanted to canter, but HoneyBee refused. At the end of the summer I was a little discouraged—all this time and no canter. My brothers tried to help me, but to no avail; she simply refused. I did keep trying though, and one day it happened quite by surprise.

From that point on I was allowed out of the pen to ride around the farm. We never stopped or looked back.

HoneyBee never cared if I had pimples on my face or that no one at school liked me; she always accepted me. We had 12 wonderful years together. One day when I got home from school—on a very cold February day—my brother came out of the barn and told me that HoneyBee was sick. He had called the vet, who was on his way. HoneyBee was in her stall in obvious agony. I tried to console her and let her know the vet was coming. She went down shortly before the vet arrived. Through my weeping I heard snatches of colic, twisted intestines and no hope. She was gone.

Twelve years passed before I was able to afford the privilege of owning another Arabian. HoneyBee lives on in my life; I am grateful to her for all that she taught me, and for introducing me to the world of Arabian horses. ♘

Connie Kurtz lives in eastern South Dakota with her husband and two boys. The family enjoys life in the country with their four Arabian horses and one pony, along with two dogs, a pygmy goat and an assortment of cats.

Thanks Doc!

By Mona P. Goldstein

For as long as he remembered, Steve Engle loved animals and knew he wanted to work with them. When he was 11 years old, he received his first horse. Sugar, a cream-colored buckskin, had a feisty personality, but the more Steve tended to her, the more manageable her behavior became and the stronger the bond grew between them.

School, particularly science and—when he was older—medicine, also gave him great pleasure. When he graduated in 1978 from Texas A&M University, Steve eagerly embraced first his internship, then his practice in veterinary medicine. Twelve to 14-hour days began early, long before daybreak, as he cared for the horses at the race-track. Then it was off to the farms, tending to his country practice, before returning once again to the track. Every day added another hundred miles of driving the well-trafficked streets of South Florida. When the busy season arrived, the time and miles increased. A thousand miles a week with only a few hours of sleep each night induced a constant state of fatigue.

As always, the rewards outweighed the struggles. Steve met some fascinating people, felt the satisfaction of bringing comfort to his patients, and traveled to interesting places. He met and married Margie Goldstein, a show jumping equestrienne who shared his passions: a love of animals, a commitment to their professions, and an ability to find joy in everything they pursued. His wife's work with show jumpers resulted in the expansion of his practice to include these prized horses that followed the riding circuit.

As Steve's treatment of show jumpers increased, so did his need to use alternative techniques. The years 1995-1996 became even busier as he pursued courses in both acupuncture and chiropractic. The value of his wide-ranging techniques would soon become apparent.

Steve has gentle hands; strong, but gentle. They are the hands of a healer, a large animal veterinarian who uses his fingers and palms to probe and question in a quest to relieve pain and minister to the good health of his patients.

Steve once received a phone call from one of his country clients. "Steve, remember the young, well-mannered Thoroughbred you treated the last time you were here? Well, T.P. has recently become totally unmanageable. No matter what I try, he's just unruly. I used to be able to ride him with no trouble at all. Now, when I ask him to do the simplest little thing, he begins to buck, veering in one direction and then in the opposite. He won't cooperate in any way. Can you help us?"

Within a short time, Steve and his assistant, Julie, were at the owner's barn. T.P. stood rigidly in his stall, his dark brown coat drenched with sweat. The normally neat hair in his black mane and tail was tangled and matted. As they approached him, T.P. snorted loudly, exposed his teeth in a threatening manner, and shot up his ears straight and stiff. Steve, recognizing the horse's apprehension, talked to him in soothing tones. "It's alright, fella. We're going to help you. Easy now. Easy, just let me look at you."

But T.P. had other ideas, and reared up suddenly,

just missing his would-be helpers. Every time Steve even approached him, T.P. would bolt up on his hind legs and kick out with his front ones. Finally, Steve was able to reach behind his neck and around his body, as he and Julie tried to hold the horse still. The horse continued kicking and resisting all of their efforts. Steve and Julie then enlisted the help of one of the barn workers, and, while the other two held the protesting animal, Steve's gentle hands probed and sought answers over T.P.'s neck, shoulders, back and haunches. From the reactions of his patient, Steve realized the horse had injured his poll. Steve massaged T.P.'s head in an effort to calm him and to gain his confidence, and then carefully adjusted the horse's neck into proper alignment.

After several minutes of this firm, gentle massaging, T.P. began to relax. His muscles lost their tension and his body no longer was rigid with pain. Steve continued manipulating the affected areas and suddenly realized that T.P. had placed his head on his benefactor's shoulder and was nickering softly.

Steve turned to his client and said, "T.P. was hurting and angry. I think he should be fine now, but call me if the pain returns."

He was relieved that no calls were necessary. A few weeks later, Steve returned to the same barn to treat another horse. T.P. was out in the pasture and, at the sound of Steve's voice, galloped over to him. He once again placed his head on Steve's shoulder and nickered softly.

Steve shook his head in amazement, laughed, and patted the expressive animal. "T.P., I've had many owners thank me, but this is the first time I've been thanked by a horse himself! It's a pleasure to see you so well again. Thank you, my friend. I needed that."

Who says animals can't talk? ☙

Mona Pastroff Goldstein wrote and published several books of a professional nature during her 35 year career as an elementary-school teacher, principal, and consultant. Now that she is retired, she has looked to her husband, Irvin, and her children, Mark, Eddie and Margie for inspiration. They haven't disappointed her! Daughter Margie Goldstein Engle, six-time winner of the AGA Rider of the Year Award, is the subject for Mona's newest book, No Hurdle Too High.

Molly

By Tannetta Dow

I bought "Molly" just over a year ago. She was very old and couldn't do any extensive work anymore, but I knew she would be perfect for my three very young children. She didn't have any registration papers, and in fact, no one knew exactly how old she was.

We all came to love Molly tremendously; out of the six horses we had, she was the only one that was just perfect, absolutely perfect. My 2, 4, and 5-year-old kids could ride her alone out around the barn, and I knew she would take care of them. My 2-year-old loved to brush her, and Molly would stand there so very patiently. My 5-year-old had his first trail ride on her, and my 4-year-old loved to sit on her while she ate. I loved her because she was so kind in spirit. It was always as if she knew that she was dealing with children, and would never even move a foot so as not to hurt or scare them.

Earlier this year, we rescued a Thoroughbred mare. Two months after we got her, she had a beautiful foal that we named Hope. When it came time for weaning, I put Hope in with Molly, and she accepted the "grandmother" role just like she did everything else—with infinite wisdom and kindness.

Late this past fall, I became greatly concerned about how Molly would fare in our cold, icy winters. She was very arthritic and beginning to lose weight. We tried everything to help her, but to no avail. Finally, with the help of my vet, my husband and some other close friends, I decided that it was in her best interest not to attempt another winter. Oh, how I cried with having to make that decision! How could I make that decision and then look into her kind, trusting eyes?

We had about a week between when the decision

was made, to the day that Molly was to be put to sleep. I cried for many hours, as we got prepared for this very sad day. Well-meaning friends told me that we had given her a wonderful last year—she had endless pastures, equine friends and a fresh stall at night—but still I cried. How do we ever make this decision and feel right about it?

My vet gave me some reassuring words. He said, "You are better off doing this two months too early than one day too late." Despite my own pain, deep in my heart I knew he was right.

The days before Molly was put to sleep were filled with tears for her and concerns for Hope. Knowing what was going to happen, I tried to separate the two for a few hours each day, and put Hope in with one of my geldings. Hope would call for Molly the entire time, and not settle down to graze or relax. On one of these days, Hope became so upset that she ran through a fence. This was clearly going to be very hard on all of us.

The day before Molly was put to sleep, my heart was so broken that I just let the two of them have their last day together. I figured Hope had enough stress, and I would just have to deal with that once Molly had passed away.

The following day the vets arrived, and I explained

to them the concerns I had for Hope. My vet suggested that once Molly had died, that I bring Hope out to "see" her. I held Molly as she died and told her over and over again how much she was loved. Then my friend Theresa and I brought Hope down to Molly, who was now lying beside her grave and let Hope smell Molly all over. She kept sniffing and in particular kept breathing into her mouth. She would sniff Molly's whole body, but always come back to her mouth, and breathe into it. After about 10 minutes she stepped away on her own accord, and started grazing. She has not called for Molly since then.

I believe something very spiritual happened that day, and my only consolation is that we gave Hope the chance to say goodbye. I saw that on some level, she understood what had happened; it was as if she registered Molly's death, and that no amount of calling would bring her back. When it was clear that Hope had her time with Molly, we put her in the pasture with one of the geldings, and she settled right down.

We lined Molly's grave with fresh boughs of evergreens, put a blanket over her and covered her with evergreens, and then built a lovely stone wall around her grave. I read a prayer at her grave, and left it there.

We renamed the field she is buried in as "Molly's field." Though I still cry often, I realize that this was right, that she is still with us in many ways, and that we were able to give her a dignified end. Though I don't know much about her history, I am sure she was worked hard. I am so glad that we gave her a peaceful retirement year. She was an ordinary horse that made an extraordinary difference in the lives of three young children, and in mine, too.

When I go out at night to check on the horses, I always pause a moment, look at the sky, and say, "Good night Molly, I love you, and thanks!" ☺

Tannetta Dow was born and raised in Holland, where she developed her love for horses as the owner of a Dartmoor pony for 34 years. Tannetta and her husband, John, live with their three young children in Hope, Maine. "A thank you to John my husband, for accepting my grief and tears, Theresa and George for being there and for all that you did, Mike and Ernie for the dignity with which you carried this out. Thank you Molly for being part of all of our lives, we are better for it."

A horse is worth more than riches.

Spanish proverb

Big Wheels

By Terry Bessette

Back in 1976, my husband and I were in Kentucky searching for show prospects and were introduced to a local dealer. The dealer invited us to his (tobacco) barn to see a big "cresty-necked" horse he had recently picked up. I can still remember the March wind blowing as we walked up the hill to the barn. The dealer opened the sliding door, and this big horse with a massive neck almost trampled us to get out of the stall. There were three horses together in that stall, the wind was whipping through, the walls were coming down, and the horses were separated from the other stalls by a few strands of wire.

This horse was a bright bay with three white socks. On his long and finely chiseled face was a strip and a snip. He stood about 16.1 hands and while that's not particularly tall, he seemed huge. It must have been his neck! Yes, his neck had a crest, and it was proportioned well, giving him a proud, stately presence.

The only place to try him was up and down on the very short driveway, with a dog yapping at his heels. I don't think he'd ever had a saddle on his back; I think he must have been a driving horse. He behaved well, but didn't have a clue about leg aids. We thought he might be a Hackney, or some kind of carriage horse. His bone, while well defined, was more substantial than the Thoroughbred; he was definitely not a Quarter Horse or any other American riding horse, and this was before the influx of warmbloods to America.

The dealer told us that the horse seemed spooky at first, so he tried to settle him down by tying a metal trash can lid to his tail! Well, he didn't spook that day, but for the rest of his life he did have a spooky streak. He'd jump any jump he was aimed at neat as a pin, but walk up to it? No way.

When we decided to buy him, the dealer assured us that Big Wheels shipped really well. In fact, he had brought the horse down from Minnesota in the back of his pickup!

Less than a year later, when he might have been doing pre-greens, Big Wheels was showing in the preliminary jumpers in Florida (back when there was only one level of preliminary). Unfortunately, he suffered an injury and his career was put on hold. But not before he caught the eye of a top jumper rider, who built jumps for us to the tops of the standards and 5'6" wide. The higher the jumps went, the tighter he folded his knees. Kind of like a pony, with his round neck and tight knees!

He was a wonderful horse that saved my life more than a few times. I remember when he was very green, we were schooling over 3'6" jumps on a three-stride line. He landed off the first jump and stumbled. His nose went to the ground, and I ended up on his neck at eye level with the second fence of the line—a big, solid coop. My husband and our farrier were watching from a distance and saw us disappear behind the coop. Big Wheels' momentum carried us forward (he was still on his knees), and I knew I was going to meet the coop head on. But somehow this horse did what he had to do, and by the time we met the coop, we were in the air jumping in fine form. His movement placed me back over the saddle, and we landed as if nothing unusual had happened!

Years later, I had a serious accident while catch-riding a horse at a show. Big Wheels was designated as my recovery horse, the horse I started back on. Later, when I needed a spinal fusion and shouldn't have been riding, he carted me around jumper courses purely on his own. I was merely a passenger, trying to minimize the pain of every move, and somehow he carried us safely around. During that time we competed in a jumper classic in Boston and placed fourth. Even though we didn't win the class, a picture of Big Wheels appeared in the Boston newspaper the following day.

Big Wheels had a lot of fans due to his kindness and unusual looks. He was an eye-catcher, with his arched neck, bright expression, ears always forward, his proud carriage, and his pony-like style over the jumps. Someone once said, "When you put the tack on that horse, it's like putting him in a tuxedo." Friends still reminisce about him, as he was always the center of attention with visitors in the barn.

Big Wheels was with us for almost 23 years. A few years before the end, we sent him to a friend's farm to be the gentleman companion of a broodmare, keeping her company in the field; of course she loved him. He came home for his final year and rests on our farm. Just a few days ago, my daughter called me from the horse show at West Palm Beach. She asked me to buy back her wonderful equitation horse when he's 25 "so he can be our next Big Wheels." 🍎

Terry Bessette began riding in the 1960s and competed as a junior rider in hunters, jumpers and equitation, and later as a professional. She became a real estate appraiser in 1987 and is now a multifamily housing appraiser for the U.S. Department of Housing and Urban Development. She lives in North Scituate, Rhode Island, where she and her husband, George, have trained hunters and jumpers from their home, Stone House Farm, since 1974. Their daughter, Devon, recently completed her junior riding career and is continuing in the family tradition with horses.

Show me your horse and
I will tell you what you are.

Old English Saying

Boston Banker

By Betsy Nye

It was in 1995, when I was 16 years old, that Boston Banker became an integral part of my life. His career has spanned nearly three decades, crossed the continent, and touched the lives of many.

A Thoroughbred born in 1973, Boston is descended from the great Man O' War through his sire. Like his famous predecessor, Boston was bred for the racetrack. He had a moderately successful career at the track, winning small races in Florida and New Jersey. But Boston's conformation was not suited for speed. It wasn't until he left the racing world for the show hunter circuit that Boston truly began to shine.

Boston was shown successfully in the pre-green hunter division, then in the first and second year greens. As legend has it, at that time Boston was sold to a rival barn and subsequently went lame. On examination, veterinarians surmised that someone—possibly a competitor—had driven a nail into the sensitive frog of Boston's hoof, cutting the head of the nail off so it would not be visible. The talented gelding came back from the injury, hinting at the strength of the spirit that would serve him well in the future.

After his green years were over, Boston was sold to a rider on the West Coast. While I have never learned exactly what he did there, several people have mentioned that they remembered him from the equitation ring in California.

Boston returned to the east after a few years and spent the next portion of his life as an equitation horse. He carried juniors to the "Big Eq" finals for several years in a row, even placing at the National Horse Show. As anyone who has spent years on the show circuit is aware, equitation courses have changed greatly over the years. When the courses became larger and trappier—more jumper-like—the slightly short-strided Boston began struggling. It was decided at this time that the gelding would be retired from the equitation ring.

In the early 1990s, Boston arrived in Vermont. Heather, his owner at that time, was a student at the University of Vermont, and Boston came to school with her as her practice horse. Heather boarded Boston at Catamount, the farm where I learned to ride.

In 1992, Boston was stricken with a serious bout of colic. Lipomas in his abdomen had cut off the blood supply to a large part of his intestine. Boston, then 19, was transported to the local veterinary hospital for surgery. Despite a grim prognosis, the horse's owners insisted that everything possible be done to save him. Veterinary surgeons removed a large, diseased portion of Boston's intestine. During surgery it was discovered that both of Boston's jugular veins were significantly damaged, most likely the result of an infection from an intravenous injection. After the surgery, the vets did not expect Boston to live through the night. The next day, however, the horse was on his feet and alert. Thanks to the wonderful care given to him, his own spirit, and a bit of luck, Boston survived.

Boston's owners then made an important decision. Knowing that the horse would be happier enjoying his semiretirement at Catamount than he would be returning to a rigorous show schedule, they donated Boston to the farm's owner. Boston thrived on the good care and consistent turnout at Catamount, and eventually went back to work. Boston's new owner used him in the lessons she taught to the UVM Equestrian Team and for a few other students. This is when I first got to know Boston.

Despite a fairly late start in riding, I became fully engrossed in the sport. In order to earn extra riding time, I worked at Catamount. Finally my parents agreed to lease a horse for me. My trainer mentioned Boston as a possibility at the time, but quickly dismissed him as too difficult for me. I leased Trooper, another Thoroughbred, and began to learn to jump. When my lease on Trooper ran out, I finally had the chance to ride Boston.

I have never been a brave rider, and thus sought a horse that would be completely honest over fences. Boston turned out to be just what I needed. This is not to say that Boston and I had a perfect relationship from day one. In fact, I spent nearly as much time on the ground during that first year as I did in the saddle! Boston would be trotting along, quietly and happily, when he would suddenly drop his inside shoulder, spin and run. He did occasionally spook for good reasons, but for the most part I think it was his way of "spicing up" flatwork. I was told that it was important to always keep him occupied.

Boston and I began showing that summer. Although he was completely honest over fences, he did have his quirks. At 22 years of age, Boston had learned how to take care of himself. He would go around the ring on a 10-foot canter stride, stepping over the fences carefully. Early in the season, my goal was to add no more than one stride in the lines—a goal I did not always achieve!

Toward the end of the summer, my courage over fences was increasing. At one show, I finally decided that we were not going to add strides in any of the lines. I came to the first fence, saw the long spot, and went for it. There is a famous quote which says, "Throw your heart over the fence, and your horse will follow." Boston, it seems, had never heard this quote. I threw my heart, and my upper body, at that long distance, and found myself on the ground. Boston had decided that the distance was far too long to be safe, and, ignoring his novice rider, had added another step. Despite all the strides we added, Boston was so smooth and consistent a jumper that we usually placed in the top three. We finished the season as reserve champions in the Special (2'6") Hunters division on the Vermont Horse Shows Association circuit.

That winter, Boston proved to me that, along with looking out for himself, he really was taking care of me as well. One cold afternoon, Boston was clowning around as usual, and bucked me off. Normally, after tossing me off, he would canter around the ring—laughing, I'm sure, in his own way. This time, when I came off, my boot became caught in the stirrup. I was lying on my back, my leg above me. Several people in the ring began to run toward me before someone ordered everyone to stand still. They shouldn't have worried. Boston stood like a soldier until someone eased up beside him and released my foot. He seemed to instinctively know that it was not the time for fun and games.

The following season, we moved up to the Children's Hunters and eventually the 3' medals. Although we still added strides occasionally, Boston and I were beginning to become a team. I could now sense his playful spooks coming, and although I couldn't always prevent them, I could usually stick them out and laugh about it. Along with competing at the local shows, I competed at the A-3 rated Vermont Summer Festival for the first time that year. While I was overwhelmed by the sheer number of competitors and by the famous names I kept hearing over the loudspeaker, Boston was in his element. In the first class of our warm-up division, Boston jumped around like a champ, earning us a second place out of more than 20 riders. I began to relax, realizing that at least one of us knew what we were doing. Our classes on Friday and Saturday went so well that my trainer and I decided that I would enter the Children's Hunter Classic on Sunday. Boston and I received an 82 on our first trip, the second highest score for that round. Our score of 76 on the second trip earned us a sixth place in the first classic of my life.

During the summer of 1996, I finally summoned the courage to take Boston around the half-mile racetrack at Catamount. He was very polite about remaining at a quiet canter, rather than bolting as I expected the retired racer to do. Then, as we approached the turn, Boston dragged me to the inside of the track, cutting the corner as close as possible. Coming out of the turn onto "the homestretch," he swapped to the outside lead and picked up the pace a bit, just as racehorses are taught. It had been almost 20 years since Boston had raced, but he still knew his job on the track as well as he knew his job in the show ring.

The final show of 1996 for us was the Vermont Horse Show Association's equitation finals. I didn't begin riding in the Medal until later in the season, and so had not had much experience with the questions posed by an equitation course. Many of the riders in my division were girls I had looked up to for years, including some who went on to perform admirably at the National Horse Show. I went into the judged warm-up convinced I could not compete seriously in such company. Thus, I was very relaxed, riding only for my own pleasure. I had the ride of my life. Boston was in front of my leg and forward, and for once my eye was working. We didn't miss a step. I left the ring ecstatic, but still certain I wouldn't place. Winning that warm-up class remains one of my proudest moments.

I continued to show Boston in the 3' classes in 1997, although I didn't compete as consistently. I was finishing my senior year of high school and preparing to start college at the University of Vermont. In June, Boston pulled a suspensory ligament in his hind leg. The vets and farrier were talking about six to 12 months of stall rest; a death sentence, in my mind, for a 24 year-old-horse.

Miraculously, less than a month later, Boston was showing again. For the third time, he had overcome a potentially career-ending injury to return to the show ring.

I wasn't able to afford to lease Boston while I was at college. I lived at home, however, and continued to exercise him several times a week for the girl who began leasing him. The next year, Catamount Farm closed down, and all the horses except for Boston were sold. Boston was leased to another girl in Vermont who was looking to move up from the ponies. I saw him at shows on and off throughout the summer, but it hurt to see someone else on the horse I loved so much.

After that season, Boston was sold to the managers of the Ox Ridge Hunt Club in Connecticut. I was devastated at first—I was certain nobody could love Boston or care for him the way I could. But as time went on, and I heard numerous positive things about Boston's new owners, I came to an important realization. As much as I loved Boston, he had taught me all that he could. It was time for someone else to learn from "the pro."

Not a day goes by that I don't think of Boston. Every horse I ride is compared to him, and the lessons I learned during my four years with Boston still help me today. When my young horse spooks and bucks me off, I remind myself that there was a time I couldn't stay on during Boston's spooks either. When I'm cantering toward a fence, I remember how much easier it was to find a spot when Boston was in front of my leg, and I push the horse forward. Having Boston to ride during the earlier years of my riding career was one of the best things that could have happened to me.

Six months after Boston left Vermont, I had a dream that Boston was hospitalized. In my heart, I felt that that this meant that my beloved equine friend had died. I later found the e-mail address for Ox Ridge, but couldn't summon up the courage to write. This was probably the closest I will come to understanding the feelings of those parents whose children run away or are abducted. I didn't know if I preferred to live with the possibility that he was still alive, or to know for certain that he had died.

Finally, in April of 2000, a friend wrote to Ox Ridge to inquire about Boston for me. It turns out that not only is Boston alive and well, but he is still working, teaching yet another young rider all the wonderful lessons he once taught me. May he continue to do so for years to come. ♘

Betsy Nye is a student at the University of Vermont, with plans to graduate in May 2001 with a degree in Animal Science. She began riding at the age of 12 and competed in the hunter and equitation divisions during high school. After leasing horses for a number of years, Betsy recently purchased her first horse, a four-year-old Hanoverian named Tristan. She plans to show Tristan in both dressage and hunters.

Living on Love

By Bonnie Kreitler

After a nationwide search by Purina Mills in 1994, Flicka was declared the oldest horse in America. Five years later at age 52, he is still owner Sara Spanial's best friend.

As a rough rule of thumb, horsemen figure one year in a horse's life is equivalent to about three in human terms. That would make Flicka 150 years old, give or take, as humans go. Although arthritis has slowed his steps, his teeth aren't what they once were and his back sags a tad, Flicka's soft coat still gleams with good health. There's a sparkle in his eye and, according to his family, he hasn't forgotten how to flirt with the ladies when an opportunity presents itself.

When the Spanials researched Flicka's history for the Purina contest, former owner Albert Brandiff did not recall how old the little 14.3-hand Cracker gelding was when he started wrangling cattle with him on a central Florida ranch. Brandiff did calculate, however, that he rode the horse for 37 years before they both retired to lives of service. Brandiff entered the seminary. Flicka entered a therapeutic riding program where he developed a reputation as a trustworthy, unflappable mount.

When the riding program disbanded seven years later, the owners called Nancy Spanial. They had heard she was looking for a bombproof horse for then six-year-old Sara to ride. Though warned that the horse was elderly, Nancy agreed sight unseen that Flicka sounded just like the horse they needed.

Young Sara had been praying for a horse. When you're asking the Lord for favors, her mother advised, it's best to be specific. So Sara prayed for a black horse with a white blaze, that was friendly and sweet. As Flicka backed off the trailer at dusk near Christmas that year, Sara was ecstatic. "He's just what I asked for!" she exclaimed. Her parents, however, were immediately worried about whether they had made the right decision. Would this gaunt animal last through the winter or break their daughter's heart?

Nancy, a former veterinary technician, immediately began making mashes for Flicka using rolled oats, sweet feed and vitamins. "Within two months we saw a huge difference," Nancy says. Flicka eventually regained over 200 pounds. The Spanials mix Flicka's Purina Senior feed with water to create a soft mash his geriatric teeth can handle. Twice daily in the summer and three times daily in winter Flicka munches mash in a stall where he can eat undisturbed. "He takes a leisurely hour and a half to eat," Nancy reports. And while he dines, Sara grooms and pampers him.

"We have always used animals to teach our children responsibility and maturity," Nancy says. Sara learned to ride on Flicka. "He took me for my first canter, my first jump," she says. "Flicka was so good. So many horses take advantage of a little kid, but he never did." Sara recalls that Flicka always picked up on what she wanted to do, even when she gave him the wrong signal. "He's sort of like your best friend or big brother. He looks after you and takes care of you."

The elderly gelding is on a regular deworming program in addition to the careful attention to his diet. "I'm a big believer in preventative maintenance," says Nancy. It helps that Flicka comes from hardy genetic stock. While the vet has stitched and treated the Spaniels' other horses over the years for various accidents and ailments, the Cracker gelding has never needed anything more than routine care.

As Sara grew taller and heavier, she stopped riding Flicka. Now she herds cows on her mom's gelding, McCloud, or patiently works to gentle the Mustang filly that the Spanial's adopted from the Bureau of Land Management. These days, Flicka mostly hangs out. Sometimes he and his buddy McCloud push the cows around the pasture just for old times sake. And he's still Sara's best friend, listening to the teen's dreams and schemes as they lean against one another under his favorite tree out in the pasture.

From the moment he stepped off the trailer, Sara never thought of Flicka as too old or too slow or too plain. As a matter of fact, when she first learned how old he was, Sara wasn't really impressed. "I didn't grasp how amazing it was," she says. Her advice to other teens wishing for a horse is to look, as she did, below the surface at what's inside. Regardless of the horse's breed or age, she says, the kind of horse an animal will be depends on the love and care he gets. "It's not about pedigrees," she says, "it's about what you make of them." ♻

*Reprinted with the kind permission of **The Horsemen's Yankee Pedlar** and Bonnie Kreitler*

*Bonnie Kreitler has been involved with horses for almost half a century and has been writing about them for the past 15 years. Kreitler Media Services based in Easton, Connecticut, provides marketing assistance for horse industry businesses. The author of **50 Careers with Horses!** published by Breakthrough Publications, Bonnie balances work with play by riding and driving her Morgan mare in the New England countryside.*

Tribute to a
Horse Show Mom

By Kimberly Gatto

It would be pointless for me to talk about horses and riding without mentioning the person to whom I owe it all—my mother, Ann Gatto. She has sacrificed much, both financially and emotionally, to support me in my love for horses.

My friends have always told me how lucky I am to have such a great mom. I couldn't agree more. From the time I discovered the sport at age 13, she took time out of her hectic daily schedule to shuttle me to the barn and to horse shows throughout New England. At one point, our house in the city was over an hour's drive from the barn where I rode. I still cannot fathom how my mom found the strength to drive such a distance, four times per day, to drop me off at the barn, return home to work, and repeat the process to pick me up later in the day. She got up with me at 3:00 a.m. on horse show days, helped me pack the car, and shuttled us both home at 10:00 p.m. after a grueling day My mom has never been an "equestrian" herself, but has always supported my passion completely. While she has what she calls "a healthy respect" for equines, she thought nothing of holding my horses, brushing their tails or patting baby powder into my grey pony's coat to ensure a glistening show-ring shine. She always reminded me that if I looked my best, I had a better chance of riding my best. She was correct.

Not only did she tend to my horses, but was often asked to hold or walk those belonging to friends, trainers, and sometimes, strangers. (We still laugh about the time I saw my mom holding onto a little girl's pony as the child took a last minute look at the course. Little did my mom know that she held the reins to the reigning Zone and National Small Pony Champion!) My mom stood out with me in rainstorms, in sweltering heat and in bitter cold as my number-one cheering section, refreshment stand and groom. Show after show, she never complained.

My mother wanted me to learn to do things myself, so she never bathed or groomed my horses for me. Those were things for which I, as the rider, was responsible. Her job was that of a helping hand, a last minute polisher, and a shoulder to cry on when things went wrong. In the subjective world of horse showing, my mother relayed to me a motto that her grandmother had taught her: "life is not fair." It is a lesson that has carried over into all aspects of my life.

My mom always reminded me to keep the sport in perspective. While I know she was thrilled each time I gained a new blue ribbon and trophy, I know that she was just as proud on my pink-and-green or "no ribbon" days. As long as the horse and I were healthy, ribbons and trophies were not a necessity. She also did me the favor of never "sugar-coating" anything. When I rode well, she commended me, but never gave me a false sense of reality. In fact, I can recall a few instances when I didn't do my best, but due to the subjectiveness of the judging system, still ended up on top of a fairly large class. In these situations, my mom light-heartedly let me know how SHE would have pinned the class.

Whenever my horses became ill or injured, my mother was there with support and comfort. She helped me boil water for a hot soak, and sat nearby while I walked my horse when she colicked from a food allergy. My mother understands what my horses mean to me, and in the process has found out how much they mean to her as well. She cried with me when my beloved mare aborted a foal, and rejoiced when I rescued a filly from slaughter. Through me, she has discovered her own love for horses.

My mother never told me how upset she was when I outgrew my large pony. It wasn't until many years later, as she gazed upon a photo of us from our first show, that she mentioned how often she thinks of him, and how she privately cried when we sold him to a younger rider. She knew how much it meant to me to move on to a horse, and worked extra hard to ensure that I got the beautiful mare that I wanted, even though her price tag was a bit above my parents' designated "spending limit."

Last year, shortly before Christmas, I made the trip to the tack store for some last-minute gifts and supplies. My mom wasn't busy that night, so I asked her if she'd like to come along. As we arrived at the store, an equestrian artist was setting up a display of horse-related jewelry. From the moment I laid eyes on it, my gaze was fixed on a small blue ribbon pendant carved entirely in silver. I knew, however, that my pre-Christmas budget wouldn't allow for such a purchase.

On Christmas Eve, my mother presented me with the tiny blue ribbon on a gilded chain. Knowing how much I had wanted that jewel, she made a special trip to the store to purchase it for me. That necklace is just one example of the bond between my wonderful mother and me.

I wear the necklace every day. ☙

About the Author

Kimberly Gatto was born and raised in Boston, Massachusetts. She first discovered horses at the age of 13 after accompanying some friends on a trail ride. That same year, she became the owner of Irish Spring, a feisty Connemara pony.

In 1985, Kim teamed up with her mare, Chutney (a.k.a. "As You Like It"), with whom she competed in AHSA hunter shows for several years. The pair recently began studying dressage. Kim plans to show both Chutney and her young Thoroughbred, Grace, in lower level dressage competitions.

An honors graduate of Wheaton College, Kim is a frequent contributor to several equine magazines including **The Chronicle of the Horse** and **Sidelines**. She is also the author of the sports biography, **Michelle Kwan: Champion on Ice** (Lerner, 1998).

DO YOU HAVE A STORY TO SHARE?

Do you have, or know of, a true horse story that would fit well into our next edition of **An Apple A Day**?

If so, please contact us at:

*Half Halt Press
P.O. Box 67
Boonsboro, MD 21712
Attention:* **An Apple A Day**

Or e-mail the author at: AppleBook2@aol.com

If your story is chosen for publication, you will receive a free copy of **An Apple A Day, Volume II**.